OVACOME
25 YEARS OF A SPECIAL CHARITY

Robert Leach

**Grosvenor House
Publishing Limited**

This book is published by
Grosvenor House Publishing Ltd
Link House
140 The Broadway, Tolworth, Surrey, KT6 7HT.
www.grosvenorhousepublishing.co.uk

A CIP record for this book
is available from the British Library

ISBN 978-1-80381-252-6

DEDICATED TO
THE MEMORY OF SARAH DICKINSON
1965 - 1997
OVACOME'S FOUNDER AND GUIDING SPIRIT

CONTENTS

FOREWORD

I feel hugely privileged to have been patron of Ovacome since the very beginning, having reached out to its founder, Sarah Dickinson, when the charity was little more than an idea that she had talked about in a magazine.

A teacher at my son's school had shown me the article in *Good Housekeeping,* in which Sarah spoke about wanting to set up a support group for everyone affected by ovarian cancer — those diagnosed, their families and friends.

The story resonated. Sarah talked about her diagnosis during her pregnancy and the impact on her family. My son, Jonathan, who was at preschool at the time, had been upset that a girl in his class had lost her mother to the disease. I was touched by what had happened and wanted to do something.

Sarah was asking other women in her position whether they would want to get involved in creating a community, to connect people affected by the disease, to talk, to help one another, and to know that they were not alone.

A diagnosis of ovarian cancer can feel quite isolating, with the disease being less prevalent than some other cancers, and at the time there was no support group for women with the disease in the UK.

I hoped that, by being patron, I might in some way perhaps help Sarah raise awareness for the charity, and I was far from being alone in wanting to join her. The inaugural bike ride, launching Ovacome just months after the article appeared, was a day of great celebration.

I remember feeling an immense sense that the occasion was the start of something really good. It was so thrilling to see Sarah's boundless energy and passion turn into a real thing: what ultimately turned out to be the UK's first ovarian cancer charity.

Much has changed since those early days of Sarah creating Ovacome from her kitchen table. The charity now employs a small team of staff and operates throughout the country. It has over 4,000 members, and it helps nearly 20,000 people every year who have been affected by ovarian cancer.

It has an annual Members' Day, regular webinars from top clinicians and online activities for members, a magazine published three times a year, a Freephone support line, and a translation service to connect with people in six community languages. It also influences policy on treatments for ovarian cancer and has close relationships with clinicians.

Perhaps most importantly, the charity has never lost the ethos of what Sarah had initially hoped to achieve: a safe, supportive and empowering community for those affected by ovarian cancer. And over the years as patron I have seen first-hand the strength that this can give to people.

All these years on, I still feel as motivated and passionate about the cause as I did when I first met Sarah. I've loved being involved – from painting my nails teal for awareness month, to filming an address from my *Call the Midwife* dressing room, complete in my Sister Julienne wimple, for an online Ovacome event. It is very easy to be able to talk about an organisation that I feel so strongly about.

A lot may have changed over the years — other ovarian cancer charities have now joined the space, and my son, who started me on my journey with Ovacome, is now an adult, working in medicine with his own child now. But with the essence of Ovacome remaining unchanged, the charity continues to retain its unique standing.

It is an extremely important support organisation, helping women, their families, carers, and now also healthcare workers as well, affected by ovarian cancer. There is nothing else like it. It was a simple, but brilliant idea that needed a Sarah Dickinson to make it happen.

Jenny Agutter OBE, patron of Ovacome.

Introduction

The story of Ovacome is a remarkable one. Started a generation ago by one lady, Sarah Dickinson, who had contracted ovarian cancer and could find little information and support for either herself or her husband, it has developed into the foremost UK support charity for anyone impacted by the disease, either directly or indirectly. Over that 25-year period (1996-2021), it has developed, adapted and flourished beyond the dreams of any one of the individuals who formed the first committee of the so called "kitchen table charity" in the summer of 1996.

I first became involved with Ovacome following the death of my grandson from a very rare form of cancer. Shortly thereafter I decided to look for a trustee role with a cancer charity and, as Ovacome was looking for two new trustees at that time and my grandson's disease had a link with a small percentage of ovarian cancers, this seemed like a good fit. It did not take me long to realise just how special Ovacome is. The level of support provided by a relatively small team is truly remarkable.

The main objective of this book is to celebrate the work and achievements of Ovacome over its first 25 years of life. In doing that, I have narrated many of the events in the charity's history that have helped to shape it into the dynamic organisation that it is today. But I wanted also to celebrate the extraordinary efforts of individuals who have made major contributions to the charity over the years. To do this I have included, throughout the book, profiles of 12 individuals and one team under the heading *"Ovacome's heroines and heroes"*. I must say immediately that these are by no means the only individuals and team that have made heroic efforts throughout Ovacome's history, far from it. But, based on my research for this book, they represent at least some of those worthy of that title. If I offend anyone by omission, I apologise in advance.

Finally, I wanted to describe, in layman's terms, some of the advances in the diagnosis and treatment of ovarian cancer that have occurred over the 25-year period. I have grouped these in the book into three chapters covering consecutive timeframes: 1996-2000, 2001-2010, 2011-2021. I hope you find them at least interesting, perhaps helpful, but please remember that nothing in those chapters, indeed throughout the entire book, should be taken as medical advice. If you have any questions or concerns about your own health, *always* seek professional medical advice.

It is inevitable that a book of this nature will contain information or descriptions that might be distressing for some. Cancer is not an easy subject. However, I hope you find the overall content at least a little uplifting. As the final chapter points out, the outlook for those with ovarian cancer has never been more promising, and the pace of improvement is accelerating. Please remember that.

Whilst I was a trustee of Ovacome for a little over two years, this book has been finalised and published after my tenure has come to an end. Whilst Ovacome has been helpful to my research, and I have quoted extensively from its various publications (for which I am grateful), it is not responsible for the contents of the book. Like all charities, Ovacome relies on donations to survive and carry out its important work. If you feel able to do so, all donations are gratefully received, just visit www. ovacome.org.uk. Thank you.

Chapter 1

BIRTH OF A CHARITY

September 15th 1996 dawned over London dry, if a little cool. Being a Sunday, many adult Londoners slept in, savouring the comfort and relief of not having to run for the bus, train, tube... Thinking of a leisurely lunch or family roast later in the day. Their teenage children, surfacing in the late morning, switched on their transistor radios and listened to the first release, titled "Wannabe", of a new girl band called the Spice Girls. Life was good, unemployment had just fallen to its lowest level in five years and later some Londoners would jump into their brand new "Ka" the latest small car to be introduced by Ford, and drive to the park for some afternoon sun and relaxation.

But for one particular lady, Sarah Dickinson, and a coterie of others who had become dedicated friends over the past few months there was little time to relax. Today was the day that Sarah and her close group were about to formally launch a new charity by completing a forty mile cycle ride from Kensington Gardens to Windsor's Alexandra Park. The event had been planned and developed in meticulous detail over the previous four months and now Sarah's dream was about to come true.

1

By 7:30am two motorcyclists were out checking the route direction signs that had been put in place the evening before. In Alexandra Park, marquees were being erected, bouncy castles set up and hundreds of balloons filled with helium. In Kensington Gardens, everything was set for the off and the atmosphere was electric. At 8am prompt, as the sun smiled down benevolently from a near cloudless sky, Sarah cut a ribbon and scores of cyclists, many of whom had travelled long distances to take part in this historic event, took a deep breath, raised a huge cheer and pressed down on their pedals to head out onto the route, forty miles to go. The launch of Ovacome, the first national charity dedicated to everyone impacted by ovarian cancer, was underway.

But the story of Ovacome did not start in September 1996, or even in May that year when the first meeting of what would become Ovacome's first committee was held in Sarah's kitchen at her home in Ealing. No, the birth of Ovacome had its roots in events that began to unfurl some four years earlier.

Ovacome's heroines and heroes - Sarah's story

The spring of 1992 was a wonderful time for Sarah. She was not yet 30 years old, married to Adrian and expecting their first child. Having graduated from Cambridge University with a degree in botany she had trained as a science teacher and then embarked on a career in environmental education. Living in France, where Adrian was studying for a Masters of Business Administration (MBA) degree at the prestigious INSEAD business school, near Fontainebleu, a short drive from Paris, she was fulfilled and happy.

During her pregnancy, Sarah suffered some medical issues which were not too concerning at the time but was advised to have them investigated once her baby was born. That happy event duly occurred on November 4th that year when a beautiful, healthy baby girl was safely delivered. Delighted parents named her Michèle, and all seemed perfect.

Completing his MBA at the end of the year, Adrian took up a management consultancy position in Germany and the family moved to Frankfurt in early 1993. Having quickly settled into their new home, Sarah decided it was time to have the further investigations recommended during her pregnancy. A scan followed and the results troubled her local doctor, although no firm diagnosis was made. Throughout the rest of that year and into the first half of 1994, Sarah had follow up investigations that became more troubling as time progressed. By the middle of 1994 the concern reached a point where Adrian and Sarah decided to return to the UK and seek further advice.

Moving initially to Ealing, they were advised to consult with the specialists at the Royal Marsden Hospital in west London and, over the next few months, a series of investigations, scans and tests were completed. The results were not what Adrian and Sarah had wished and hoped for and by the autumn, a diagnosis of ovarian cancer had been made.

As with any diagnosis of cancer, the news was initially devastating but the "good news" in Sarah's case was that the cancer was first diagnosed as a slow growing germ cell type and that she had possibly ten years of active life ahead. Time to enjoy and, perhaps, even time for more effective treatments to provide a cure or, at least, to prolong life further. But, as so often in life a further, cruel twist was to come.

A further consultation was scheduled for a few weeks later and on this occasion a different and more junior doctor was seen. The news was worse and the junior doctor appeared nonplussed that Adrian and Sarah did not have the facts that he had: her cancer was far more aggressive and, in fact, was terminal. She had one to two years of life left; the devastation was complete.

Sarah launched into the first round of chemotherapy and, throughout 1995, underwent several surgical procedures, including one to reroute her bowel. Unfortunately, her cancer did not respond to the initial treatment and in early 1996 she underwent further chemotherapy, including one cycle of a triple drug regime with the objective of at least slowing down the advance of the disease. Always positive, Sarah undertook various further treatments in her attempt to combat the disease but none of them was to have a lasting effect.

Sarah's own mother had died when she was five years old and Sarah was acutely conscious that Michèle would have to face the same experiences that she had had to deal with. To ease this burden on Michèle, with great courage and love, Sarah wrote a book of memories for her, including many stories and photographs. Sarah's ultimate goal was to celebrate Michèle's fourth birthday with her and Adrian and this she achieved in November that year. Sadly, it was to be the final birthday celebration as Sarah's disease continued to advance and she succumbed to it in April 1997.

The stark story of Sarah's cancer experience and tragic death at such a young age – just 32 – hides a reality of a strong-willed woman determined to raise awareness of this particular disease and to help others who contracted it in the future. Shortly after the final diagnosis and prognosis, Sarah and Adrian redoubled their efforts to find information not only about the disease itself but what they could do to mitigate its effects, both physical and emotional. They were disappointed by what they discovered; in fact, the amount of information available at the time, especially for younger persons with ovarian cancer, was minimal. For a time, Sarah and Adrian felt very alone.

Throughout much of 1995, Sarah's search for information and support groups continued in parallel with her gruelling treatment but was met with little success. One exception was Macmillan Cancer Support, the overarching cancer charity that provides information across a wide range of different cancer types. But Sarah was looking for something more focused, more directly relevant to her experience and that of others in a similar situation.

More happily, this quest was punctuated in the spring of that year with Sarah, Adrian and Michèle setting off in April to fulfil a long held ambition to sail the Greek islands. The voyage provided some much needed respite from the rigours of chemotherapy and helped to distract from the illness. But the cancer was never far away, with

Sarah experiencing sickness and headaches on many days. Whilst doing everything they could to cling to the joy of being together as a family, sailing from one idyllic spot to another, by July it was clear that they needed to return to London, to doctors and hospitals and treatment.

By the end of the year Sarah felt that she had exhausted her search for support groups and that, if anything was going to emerge, she would have to take the initiative herself. The germ of an idea to set up a group, maybe a charity, began to take shape and, early in the new year, Sarah began to bring together a small group of friends and colleagues to share thoughts and sound out ideas for an ovarian cancer support group. Fortunately, some of those friends had connections with the media and it was decided to explore the possibility of creating some much needed publicity through interviews and articles.

Within just a few weeks, Sarah had been invited to an interview with a journalist from *Good Housekeeping* magazine. They met, talked and Sarah's love, joie de vivre and determination to help others spilled out onto the page in what was to become a seminal article published in February 1996. Several further articles appeared in other publications, including *The Mirror Women*, and Sarah appeared on the BBC's *Good Morning* programme (together with Michèle) and Sky One. But the *Good Housekeeping* piece was the most effective. Towards the end of that article, Sarah had postulated the setting up of a support group and asked any who had an interest to contact her (via an address set up by the magazine; no internet in 1996), triggering an almost overwhelming response from sufferers, families and friends of sufferers and health professionals. Sarah's long held ambition was taking shape and Ovacome was quickly becoming a reality.

Energised by the response to her "mini publicity campaign", Sarah, with the support of her still quite informal group of friends and collaborators, prepared and launched the first ever newsletter of Ovacome, which appeared in the spring of 1996. Barely five pages long, the newsletter included some tips on dealing with cancer, a couple of personal stories and the first mention of what was to become one of Ovacome's enduring initiatives, "Fone-Friends". One of the personal stories was penned by Grace Sheppard, wife of the then Bishop of Liverpool (and ex-England test match cricketer), the Right Reverend and Right Honourable David Sheppard. Grace wrote movingly of her own experience of being diagnosed with and surviving ovarian cancer and provided enthusiastic support for Sarah's initiative. But perhaps the starkest sentence in that first newsletter, which invoked the response to her GH article, was the following from Sarah: "I have had letters from women who have gone through diagnosis, surgery and chemotherapy without meeting another women with ovarian cancer. This is a terrifyingly lonely experience". This poignant, even heartbreaking sentence struck a chord with many readers. Sarah had unleashed a movement.

Further organisation of the fledgling charity followed rapidly. On Saturday 4th May 1996, the first meeting of what had been humorously labelled "The Kitchen Table Charity" was held at Sarah and Adrian's home in Ealing. For such a new endeavour, it was a large group of enthusiastic followers with no less than ten attendees present and anxious to be involved. A committee was formed, with Sarah as the first chairperson and each of the other attendees taking on roles such as treasurer, fundraising and promotions coordinator and newsletter and Fone-Friends coordinator. Everyone present had a place and a role.

Having established the committee there was no time to waste and further important issues were discussed and decisions taken. First, the purpose of the charity was set out: "To be a nationwide support group for all those concerned with ovarian cancer, to raise awareness of the condition, to provide information, to link sufferers and to share personal experiences". Second, the constitution was discussed and it was agreed that Sarah, together with Sarah Legg (a legal professional who had been appointed as "charitable status and constitution coordinator") would work together to produce an initial draft for circulation to the committee and approval at the first annual general meeting. Next it was agreed that the newsletter was extremely important as a means of promulgating the proposed charity; that it should be published quarterly; contain both serious and more light-hearted articles and comments; attract contributions from a broad range of individuals, including those in the medical profession and provide links to other charities and support groups that may be helpful to sufferers, their families and friends. Naturally, fundraising and promotion was another critical topic. In addition to the more usual ideas, such as sponsored runs, rowing sessions, lunches – all of which could be held regionally and regularly – an animated discussion, led by Sarah, was held about holding a formal launch event in the late summer. Several possibilities were raised and debated but finally the group settled on a sponsored bike ride from Hyde Park to Windsor, passing the Royal Marsden hospital (one of the UK's major cancer hospitals) and finishing with a celebratory party, hopefully attended by some celebrity figures to help raise the profile of the event and garner media interest. Alexandra Dargie, a member of the committee who had earlier been appointed as fundraising and promotions coordinator, stepped up to take responsibility for arranging the event. Finally the committee agreed to try to attract a well-known personality to be patron of the charity once set up. Several names were discussed but the topic was left for a future date. The meeting closed with all feeling happy that a great deal of progress had been made.

Ovacome's heroines and heroes - Alexandra Dargie's story

Alexandra's willingness to join the founding committee of Ovacome, accept the role of fundraising and promotions coordinator and take on the significant challenge of organising the planned launch event highlighted her deeply felt regard for both the proposed charity and Sarah personally. This regard and enthusiasm had already produced tangible results as, some weeks earlier, Alexandra and one of her friends, Pascale, had undertaken a sponsored bike ride from Lands' End to London, taking eight days to complete and raising well over £1000, making her one of the first to raise funds for Ovacome through personal efforts. In an article published in Ovacome's second newsletter (summer

1996) she wrote: "Having read Sarah Dickinson's GH article on her feelings of her life, her family and her imminent death, I felt so inspired and determined to promote her cause and to help her set up Ovacome. A friend and I decided to cycle from Lands' End to London to raise awareness and funding." She went on to describe the journey and outline how a child in her class at school (she was a teacher), whose mother had died from ovarian cancer, had been a further motivation to complete the ride when the going got tough. She concluded her article with these words: "We would like to extend our thanks to all those supporters, families and friends who have given their time, money and support to Ovacome... But most of all we must thank Sarah who is such an inspiration and whose strength and courage has helped and enriched the lives of so many people."

Alexandra was elected chair of Ovacome in July 1996 as Sarah's health deteriorated and went on to play an important role, along with other committee members, in arranging and holding Ovacome's launch event in September. She remained as chair for more than a year, at which point she married and, with her new husband, took off for a six-month adventure around the world. However, less than one year later, now as Alexandra Whates, she returned to Ovacome to take on the newly created role of chief administrator, the first employee of the charity.

The first meeting of the kitchen table charity committee was followed swiftly by the first Annual General Meeting (AGM) of Ovacome. Held at the Manor House of Chessington World of Adventures on the 7th July 1996 it was attended by nearly 100 people, an astonishing number for a charity that had not yet been formally established and had been first suggested in a magazine article only five months earlier. The main business of the AGM was to approve the constitution that had been prepared by Sarah Dickinson and Sarah Legg and subsequently reviewed by the committee members. Approval was obtained and Ovacome was now able to apply for charitable status; a key milestone had been achieved.

Several other important initiatives were launched or progressed at the AGM. First, Fiona Richards, a general practitioner (GP), member of the committee and informal medical advisor to the charity, agreed to take responsibility for raising awareness of ovarian cancer amongst GPs and the broader medical profession. Sadly, in the mid-nineties, awareness in the profession was quite low, resulting in those with symptoms often making several visits to a doctor before proper investigations were carried out and a diagnosis confirmed. It was a founding goal of Ovacome to change this and as part of this initiative, it was agreed to produce and distribute information leaflets to GPs. The medical profession information campaign was rolling.

Second, Alexandra Dargie outlined the plans for the launch event, now firmly fixed for the 15th September. She emphasised what an exciting and momentous day this would be and asked for support in arranging and managing the many activities that were planned and in gaining publicity and media attention for the day. She was not to be disappointed.

Thirdly, the meeting turned its attention to another and, perhaps, the most important founding goal of Ovacome; the support of those diagnosed with ovarian cancer, their family and close friends, through contact with others with similar experiences. As she had written in that first newsletter, Sarah had suffered personally from this "disease loneliness" and was determined that she would be the last to do so. To help fill this void, Sarah had raised, in the first newsletter, the idea of fellow sufferers and supporters coming together in an informal network to provide friendship and companionship to each other. She could not have predicted the level of response she received. It was overwhelming and within weeks of the newsletter's publication, people across the country were talking to each other by telephone, sharing experiences and coping mechanisms and providing mutual support. Fone Friends was born. At the inaugural meeting of the kitchen table committee in May, Sharon Eastward, another of the members, had agreed to take responsibility for promoting and managing this crucial initiative and she now took to the floor of the AGM to explain the concept and to outline the progress made. It was impressive to say the least. Within a couple of months, Fone Friends had been organised into a group of nine regions across the country, each with its own regional coordinator. Within each region, a small group of Fone Friends volunteers formed the bedrock of the network, taking calls from anxious sufferers, husbands, mothers, close friends, all searching for information, reassurance, or both. It was already a lifeline to many.

The first AGM had been a great success; passionate, invigorating, determined. It was obvious that there was a great demand and a real need for a charity focused on ovarian cancer alone with the goals and objectives that Ovacome espoused. For too long this had been a silent cancer. That was about to change. But first the charity launch had to be concluded.

Around noon on September the 15th, the first cyclists to set off from Hyde Park, some three or four hours previously, began to arrive at Alexandra Park, Windsor. A little tired and saddle-sore but exhilarated to have made the journey. They were greeted by well over one hundred supporters of Ovacome who had travelled to Windsor, together with their families and friends to greet them. The sun beamed down and the party was ready to get into full swing.

Opening the festivities, Jenny Agutter, the well-known British actress, made a speech full of encouragement and enthusiasm for Ovacome's aims. Jenny's son attended the school that Alexandra Dargie taught at and knew of the death from ovarian cancer of the mother of one of Alexandra's other pupils and wanted to help. She was soon to be appointed as Ovacome's patron. Further speeches were made by two eminent gynaecological oncologists, Martin Gore of the Royal Marsden hospital and Ian Jacobs of the Royal London hospital, followed by John McGowan, Chairman of Research Ovarian Cancer, a related charity. Each of these dedicated professionals were strong supporters of Sarah and Ovacome and gave informative and interesting talks.

Speeches over it was time for fun. Cycle rides had been arranged for the children and hundreds of helium-filled balloons pulled on their strings, vainly hoping to escape to the sky. Another wonderful attraction for the younger folk were the bouncy castles which had been erected and provided endless fun for the entire afternoon. An entertainer held another group of children, seated on the grass as the sun beat down, spellbound with his stories, jokes and tricks.

The adults, whilst not secretly watching the children's entertainer, were able to enjoy the more genteel pastime of afternoon tea and browse the many stalls that had been set up to complete the fete-like atmosphere. What a wonderful afternoon was had by all! As Alexandra Dargie wrote in her chairperson's column of the winter 1996 newsletter, "The atmosphere was tremendous and it was a resounding success". As important, the event had created much publicity and raised substantial funds through sponsorship of the cyclists, sale of teas and products and donations.

Finally, fully, formally, Ovacome was launched.

Chapter 1A

DIAGNOSIS AND TREATMENT – A BRIEF HISTORY. THE 1990s

Diagnosis:

The history of diagnosis of ovarian cancer is not a particularly happy one. Ovacome's early newsletters contain moving accounts from many who had been misdiagnosed or diagnosed only after numerous visits to their doctor. The fact was that in the 1990s ovarian cancer, being a relatively uncommon occurrence, was not well understood by many in the medical profession. This had been recognised at Ovacome's first annual general meeting where Fiona Richards, a GP present, agreed that awareness was too low and proposed, together with Ruth Payne, another of Ovacome's early volunteers and a nurse, a plan of information dissemination to widen and improve knowledge and understanding of both GPs and hospital doctors.

As many women who have contracted ovarian cancer can testify, the accurate diagnosis of the disease has always been challenging. In fact there is, to this day, no simple blood test or examination that can confirm the disease or otherwise. And just to complicate matters the symptoms of early stage ovarian cancer are often similar to other, less serious, conditions.

Looking back to the early to mid-1990s the most commonly used diagnostic tools for a suspected first occurrence of ovarian cancer were medical and family history, a physical examination of the pelvic region and an ultrasound scan. Ultrasound (sonography), had been invented much earlier in the century but it was a development in the later 1950s that firmly established the technique for helping to diagnose ovarian cancers. In 1958 a paper was published in The Lancet written by two doctors, Ian Donald and John McVicar, together with an engineer, Tom Brown, titled "The investigation of abdominal masses by pulsed ultrasound". The three authors had collaborated with an engineering company to produce the world's first ultrasound scanning machine called the Diasonograph and whilst the images were crude and in two dimensions (2D) only, the era of ultrasound diagnostics was firmly established.

Whilst the early ultrasound scanning machines were large and unwieldy, rapid advances in sonography delivered much better and smaller machines. Such was the pace of change that by the mid-1980s, the portable, transvaginal sonography (TVS) machine had been introduced and by the mid-1990s it was a well-established technique. TVS allowed doctors to examine images of the ovaries and surrounding tissue more closely and in more detail than ever before. Whilst a significant advance, TVS had a drawback in that it could determine abnormal masses in *and around the ovaries but it could not reliably distinguish between benign and malignant cysts or tumours.*

One further obstacle regarding the use of ultrasound in the 1990s was that GPs could not directly refer a patient for an ultrasound scan; they had to arrange an initial appointment with a hospital consultant who would make that referral if deemed necessary.

Three other forms of scan were also available in the early to mid-1990s: computerised tomography (CT); magnetic resonance imaging (MRI) and positron emission tomography (PET). CT scanning was helpful in identifying metastatic disease but less so for early stage malignancy as it could not identify small tumours. MRI had only a small part to play in diagnosis and then usually with other techniques and tests. PET provided more detail of where the cancer was most present and how aggressive it was.

In addition to these examinations and scans, a discovery made in 1984 aided the diagnostic process. The discovery was that a protein, known as CA-125, was often elevated in those patients with ovarian cancer. Whilst an important indicator, or "tumour marker", of ovarian cancer, CA-125 levels could also be raised by much less serious conditions, for example, fibroids or even by natural processes such as menstruation. Equally, some patients with early stage ovarian cancer did not have a raised CA-125 level. Alone it was not (and still is not) a definitive guide to the presence of the disease.

Overall, in the 1990s, physical examination, TVS ultrasound scanning (sometimes supported by other types of scan) and CA-125 testing were the most prevalent forms of diagnostic procedure and initial, if tentative, diagnosis. To obtain a confirmed diagnosis, plus the classification of stage (how far the cancer had spread) and grade (level of aggressiveness) required the surgical procedure known as a biopsy (the removal of tissue and examination under a microscope), sometimes carried out as a single procedure but often as part of the surgery to remove the ovary and any adjacent malignant tissue.

Whilst not a diagnostic indicator the discovery, in the mid-1990s, that mutations in two genes (a gene is a basic building block of life) known as BRCA 1 and BRCA 2 put those with these abnormalities at more risk of developing ovarian cancer (and also breast cancer) was a crucial medical advance. These gene mutations are hereditary and subsequently it was discovered that their presence increased the possibility of developing ovarian cancer by 50% - 85% and that up to 25% of those who developed the disease had such genetic histories.

Perhaps the most important result of this discovery was that it allowed those with the mutations to be very alert to symptoms, to seek more regular screening and physical examinations, and gave them a basis to make an informed decision as to whether to opt for pre-emptive surgery to remove the ovaries, breasts or both; one of the most important and difficult decisions anyone could have to take.

Treatment:

Fortunately, the history of the treatment of ovarian cancer is more positive than for diagnosis.

Since the late 1970s, surgery to remove as much of the malignancy as possible (hopefully all of it) usually with follow up combination chemotherapy regimens, had been in place. At that time, the often-used chemotherapy was a four-drug combination known as HEXACAF. This had been found to be more effective than the previous, one-drug treatments, extending survival of advanced ovarian cancer by up to 12 months.

A significant step forward came at the end of the 1970s with the introduction of a platinum-based drug: cisplatin. Quite quickly, cisplatin was being administered in combination chemotherapies for the treatment of newly diagnosed and persistent disease. Unfortunately, through the 1980s, cisplatin was found to have quite serious side effects and it was eventually replaced, in the late 1980s and early 1990s, by another platinum based drug, carboplatin, which had a similar impact on the disease but fewer side effects.

And then, in 1992, the next significant improvement in treatment arrived through the introduction in the USA of a new class of drugs called taxanes. Derived from the bark of the yew tree (initially Pacific yew but later European yew also) taxanes had been researched for many years and early clinical trials of its effect in treating cancer had commenced in the mid-1980s. By the early 1990s, the pharmaceutical company, Bristol Myers Squibb (BMS) had, somewhat controversially, gained a near monopoly of production of the drug paclitaxel, commercially marketed as taxol.

Paclitaxel was licenced and became available through the NHS in some parts of the country (and privately) in 1996 but the high cost of the drug meant that some health authorities did not offer it – the so called "postcode lottery". In 1999, one Ovacome member, Jackie O'Donnell, played a significant role in getting paclitaxel offered under the NHS, for the initial treatment of ovarian cancer, in the Teeside health region. Finally, the National Institute for Clinical Excellence (NICE) which had been established only the previous year, approved the drug for nationwide use by the NHS in early 2000.

Paclitaxel was shown to be effective in patients with advanced disease that had stopped responding to other drug treatments, reducing tumour size by as much as half in many cases. A further breakthrough came in 1996 when the results of an advanced clinical trial demonstrated that combining paclitaxel with platinum-based drugs (initially cisplatin but later carboplatin) improved survival rates in those with advanced disease by as much as a year or more in some cases. This combination chemotherapy is still in use in the 2020s.

In 1996, at about the time that Ovacome was being formed, a drug known as topotecan was introduced. Topotecan was a new type of drug class known as "topoisomerase I inhibitors" which reduced the ability of cancer cells to divide and grow. The pharmaceutical company, SmithKline Beecham (SB), entered the market with a drug named Hycamtin which was approved for use in the UK, for recurrent or platinum-resistant ovarian cancer, later in 1996. Based partly on this development, SB became an early sponsor of Ovacome. Hycamtin had its own set of side effects, some potentially quite serious and, around the turn of the century, a further drug, liposomal doxorubicin, was seen to be as effective as topotecan but with fewer side effects. Like topotecan, doxorubicin interfered with the ability of cancer cells to divide and grow. However, it was different in that the drug itself was "wrapped" in two layers of other compounds which enabled the drug to be released much closer to the site of the tumour. Neither topotecan or doxorubicin was a cure but they represented important steps forward in the treatment of recurrent or platinum-resistant disease during the later 1990s, extending the lives of many sufferers by months or even years.

Chapter 2

GETTING THE MESSAGE OUT

The huge excitement and enthusiasm created by the formal launch event spurred efforts to progress the charity's founding objectives of helping sufferers to feel less alone and to raise awareness of the disease within both the public and the medical profession; the first task was *to get the message out.*

One of the mainstays of the "less alone" objective was the rapid development of the Fone Friends initiative. Under the guidance of Sharon Eastwood, one of the initial committee members, Fone Friends continued to expand its network of volunteers willing to speak with fellow sufferers and by early 1997 covered much of England and Wales. Representation in Northern Ireland and Scotland was to follow by the summer, an astonishing rate of expansion.

Following the second AGM of the charity, once again held in the Manor House at Chessington World of Adventures in the summer 1997, a new and larger committee had been formed and four task forces set up, the Fone Friends programme being one of those four. By late summer 1997, the network had increased to 16 geographical areas, each with an area co-ordinator and over 70 Fone Friends volunteers spanning the country. Such was the success that a mini newsletter was introduced, sent to Fone Friends co-ordinators and volunteers only.

A strategy review in May 1998 led to more progress in the summer with the appointment of "Frontline Fone Friends". Each of these volunteers had been members of the Fone Friends team for some time and had either prior experience of counselling or were given basic training. Available seven days a week, they operated on a rota system to ensure that two volunteers were on call at any given time. Whilst providing direct support to callers they also introduced them to their appropriate area co-ordinator for further one to one support.

The spring of 1998 saw a change in leadership as Sharon Eastwood, who had effectively launched and championed the network for two years, stepped down from her role. She was replaced by Karyn Connor, a young member of the charity's committee, who had developed ovarian cancer in her mid-twenties and had been the Fone Friends area co-ordinator for London. Karyn quickly brought the Frontline Fone Friends and area co-ordinators together for a seminal event over a weekend in London; for many of these volunteers it was the first time they had met although they had all spoken on the telephone many times and felt they knew each other. The event included presentations from senior oncologists, a seminar to exchange experiences and ideas for further improvement and a full day training programme in telephone counselling techniques. The goal of bringing the Fone

Friends initiative to a consistent level of support had been achieved.

Over the next two years, the Fone Friends network continued to develop and provide invaluable support to all sufferers of ovarian cancer. Not only sufferers but also their partners, as one of the first Fone Friends, Ruth Payne, testified. Ruth, a nurse who had had the disease, took telephone calls at home (Ovacome had no office at that time) and recalls speaking to a man whose wife had a very similar type of cancer to her own. The man was in floods of tears but Ruth talked to him about her own experience and successful treatment and remembers how this particular husband was much calmer and reassured by the end of the call. A very rewarding experience.

Eire was added as a new and final area in the summer of 1999, taking the total number to 18. In some areas the network developed beyond telephone support to include events and meetings of members. One notable example (not the only) was the north-east area where members met monthly in Newcastle-upon-Tyne for coffee mornings, held a Christmas lunch and even organised a sponsored fun run/jog/walk that involved not only members of the Fone Friends group but staff from local hospitals and the "fit and healthy" from local gyms! Under the guidance and formidable energy of Margaret Borthwick the north-east area was to become one of the leading lights of the programme over the next few years.

Fone Friends was clearly successful, but that success came at some human cost. First, the interactions were often physically and/or emotionally draining for the counsellors, many of whom were living with their own cancer or knew that there was a possibility that their disease may recur. Second, inevitably and sadly, some counsellors and those being counselled died, an outcome made all the more poignant by the fact that many had become friends during the process. These difficulties weighed on the programme and turnover of volunteers, including area co-ordinators, was sometimes quite high.

Karyn Connor moved back to her native Scotland in the autumn of 1999 and continued to lead the programme from there until the summer of 2000 at which point she stepped down. She had held the role for more than two years, developing the programme into a more effective and cohesive initiative that was deeply valued by all.

Over the next two years, the Fone Friends programme was managed by members of Ovacome's staff and continued to provide its services as usual; but by late 2002 it was becoming clear that the programme needed renewal. At a Fone Friends study day held in May 2003 the challenge of finding enough area co-ordinators was discussed, together with a wish by many of the volunteers to have a broader role in supporting the charity and its members. Following much deliberation, a decision was taken to wind down the Fone Friends programme and to introduce a new, wider role, that of regional Ovacome co-ordinators, or ROCs. This decision was formalised at the AGM held in September of that year.

Over a seven-year period, Fone Friends had been, in many ways, the beating heart of the charity, certainly in terms of supporting members. It had provided information, support, reassurance and comfort to hundreds, if not thousands, of sufferers and their loved ones. The essence of Fone Friends could be summarised as "sufferers supporting other sufferers". Individual volunteer counsellors did not provide medical advice, although they could direct members to appropriate sources of such advice. Their greatest impact was their ability to share experiences and empathise with what another human being was going through; to assure the individual on the other end of the telephone that they were not alone, that others had and were experiencing the same challenges, concerns, fears and successes. Through this process, many of the charity's members, plus their family and/or friends, no longer felt alone, just as Sarah had wished.

Fone Friends was not the only initiative to help support members of the charity in those early years. Information leaflets, covering various topics relating to ovarian cancer, were prepared and posted to members as required. This work stepped up to a new level in the autumn of 1997 with the production of an ovarian cancer "information pack" funded by a grant from the pharmaceutical company SmithKline Beecham (SB). The pack contained booklets and factsheets relating to a broad range of issues connected to ovarian cancer. Written by a consultant oncologist and supplemented by input from the charity's members, the pack was available to all for a modest fee covering packing and postage. Again, with the support of SB, the pack was made available to cancer centres and hospitals throughout the country, and they were encouraged to pass them (together with membership forms for Ovacome) to patients as they saw fit. A few months later the pack was supplemented by a video, introduced by Jenny Agutter, Ovacome's patron, featuring three members (and sometimes their partners) talking about their own experience of ovarian cancer.

Together, the pack and videos were a major step forward in information dissemination.

Ovacome also promoted relevant information leaflets from other sources. Just one example was the promotion, in the winter 1996 newsletter, of a leaflet from Cancer Relief Macmillan titled "Gynaecological Cancers: How to Help Yourself". The leaflet outlined six questions (agreed by the British Gynaecological Cancer Society) that every woman diagnosed with ovarian cancer should ask:

Will I have:

1. The opportunity of prompt referral to a consultant led team specialising in the diagnosis and treatment of gynaecological cancers?
2. Full discussion about options such as surgery, radiotherapy and chemotherapy before treatment starts?
3. Surgery performed by a gynaecologist who has a special interest in gynaecological cancers?
4. Radiotherapy and chemotherapy undertaken by staff with a special interest in gynaecological cancers?
5. Access to a specialist nurse or counsellor and a symptom control (palliative care) team?
6. Information on support services for myself and my partner?

In the 2020s, the answers to these questions may seem self-evident but this was not always the case in the 1990s.

The newsletter had been introduced in the spring of 1996 and remains to this day one of the most important conduits of information, members' stories and support.

Since the beginning, it had been produced and distributed, mostly on a quarterly basis, to all members wishing to receive it. Fittingly, the winter 1996 edition carried on its front page, for the first time, the charity's guiding mantra:

"Ovacome is a nationwide support group for all those concerned with ovarian cancer, involving sufferers, families, friends, carers and health professionals.

It aims to:

- Share personal experiences
- Link sufferers
- Provide information on treatments, screening and research
- And raise awareness of the condition."

This simple but powerful mantra appeared on the front page of every newsletter for the next ten years.

In parallel with Fone Friends, the introduction of information leaflets, and the quarterly publication of a newsletter, other actions were taken shortly after the inaugural AGM to progress another of the founding objectives: to raise awareness of ovarian cancer amongst the medical profession. At that AGM Fiona Richards, a GP, had agreed to take responsibility for this initiative and within a month or so information leaflets were being produced and distributed to GP surgeries. This was further supplemented by the ovarian cancer information pack once it became available.

Similar to the Fone Friends initiative, "objectives and raising awareness" became one of the four task forces established in 1997 to drive that element of the charity's strategy forward, initially under the leadership of Louise Bayne, a midwife, and then, in the autumn of 1999, when Louise became chairperson of the charity, under Ruth Payne, a practice nurse.

Ovacome's influence within the medical profession took on renewed impetus in the spring of 1997 when the charity launched a project on behalf of the Department of Health to better understand cancer patients' needs of their GPs and primary care team. Many of Ovacome's (by then more than 700) members responded by completing questionnaires expressing their views and this helped to shape future medical services.

At a more direct level, within a year or so of the launch of the charity, Ovacome staff, volunteers and members were being invited to a range of medical seminars and conferences. One of those early campaigners was Debbie Howells, the wife of then Tottenham Hotspur (and later Southampton) footballer, David Howells and, as events were to show, an excellent communicator and advocate of Ovacome.

Ovacome's heroines and heroes: Debbie Howells story

In the early to mid-1990s Debbie and her husband, David, were trying to have a baby but without success. Debbie decided to undergo investigations for potential fertility problems but was advised that all was normal and to let nature take its course. Unfortunately, all was not normal and in September 1995, Debbie collapsed and an emergency operation was carried out to remove an ovary due to a ruptured cyst. One week later, Debbie was told that the cyst was malignant. She was 26 years old.

Numerous further tests and scans were completed at which point Debbie received a positive prognosis and was asked to return for a further laparoscopy in the spring of 1996. That procedure identified that the cancer had spread to her womb and she underwent a full hysterectomy a few weeks later. Surgery was followed by six months of very intensive chemotherapy, including the drug paclitaxel, which was very new in the UK at that time. In common with many sufferers, Debbie experienced a full range of side effects, including full hair loss. She required frequent injections to boost her blood counts and, at the end of the treatment, several blood transfusions.

Throughout that period, Debbie kept herself as positive as possible by focusing on a specific aim, the immediate one to enjoy Christmas. Over the next nine months, Debbie was not well enough to work and began to think of what she could do to raise awareness of ovarian cancer and help others in similar situations. David, being a well-known footballer, had frequent media attention and Debbie realised that she was able to use this to her advantage. Over the following 18 months, she took several opportunities to talk openly about ovarian cancer and her own experience of the disease, diagnosis and treatment; always stressing the importance of a positive attitude and that life does go on. Debbie's research and interest in ovarian cancer inevitably brought her into contact with Ovacome and in the summer of 1997, she joined the committee with a particular focus on raising awareness of the disease.

Debbie and others of the then committee understood that Ovacome had to communicate directly with medical practitioners if they were to expand and reinforce their knowledge and awareness of ovarian cancer. And one of the best means of doing that was to talk to them, preferably through events. One of the first such events took place in the winter of 1997 when Debbie and Margaret Yarwood, another member of the committee, attended a meeting of 100 health professionals on the topic of ovarian cancer. In the afternoon workshop sessions, Debbie gave a talk from "the patient's perspective". As Margaret commented at the time: "It was the best session of the day. Debbie's honesty, courage and humour were very well received and many attendees left the day clutching Ovacome leaflets and newsletters". Ovacome's reputation was climbing.

By the spring of 1998 the medical professional events were in full swing and, in addition, Debbie had taken on the role of editor of the newsletter. Throughout the autumn and winter of 1997 and all of 1998, Debbie, sometimes with others, spoke, appeared or presented at a wide range of media events in the UK, Europe and, via a live press link-up, the USA. As a result, Ovacome featured several times in national newspapers, magazines, radio programmes and television channels. The joint press conference with the USA media reported the results of trials of paclitaxel (Taxol) in the UK, a very hot topic at the time. Debbie had been promoting the use of paclitaxel for some time and the latest trials had demonstrated that, in combination with cisplatin or carboplatin, as a first line treatment, the drug was very effective in prolonging survival rates. In the newsletter of summer of that year, Madeleine Gold, one of Ovacome's committee members who had joined Debbie in the press conference, gave an account of the trials and urged sufferers and their families to speak with their medical team about the use of paclitaxel in their treatment plan. This was just another example of Ovacome in action, raising awareness and supporting sufferers and their families.

Over the next three years Debbie devoted much of her energies to preparing, collating and editing the newsletter whilst continuing to support the raising awareness initiative. Additionally, in December 1998, she stood in as the charity's administrator for six months whilst Alex Whates, then the permanent administrator, was on maternity leave.

Throughout the latter part of her time working with the charity, Debbie and her husband, David, had been fostering children and, in 2000, they had the joy of welcoming a baby girl of their own into their lives via a surrogate mother. A couple of years later, they added a son through adoption.

Debbie left Ovacome reluctantly in late 2001 to focus her energies on her family but continued to support the charity and to be active in other ovarian cancer initiatives. A wonderful contribution to Ovacome and the cause of ovarian cancer sufferers everywhere.

Another initiative introduced by Ovacome that was to become a great success in raising awareness of the disease was the "adopt a hospital" scheme. Launched by Louise Bayne at the annual general meeting in the summer of 1998, the idea was simple: members were asked to "adopt" the hospital they were attending for treatment of their cancer with an initial target set to reach 50 hospitals. Very soon, many members were distributing posters, leaflets, newsletters and membership forms to display in hospital cancer patient waiting areas. In some cases these members were able not only to distribute written material but to speak with staff and sometimes make presentations. Through this activity many more sufferers were made aware of the support and information available to them and hospital staff were more informed of the patients' view of all aspects of the disease. By the winter of 1998, just a few months after launch, the target of 50 hospitals had been achieved, another key milestone reached. Over the next couple of years that number was to rise to over 100 hospitals.

Amongst the hospitals supporting Ovacome's efforts was the Royal Marsden in London, the centre that Sarah Dickinson had been treated at and one of the world's leading cancer research and treatment locations. In the summer of 1997, the hospital agreed to host an Ovarian Cancer Resource Centre at its West London site. The centre displayed information from both the hospital and the charity and was officially opened by Ovacome's patron, Jenny Agutter, in September, one year after the charity's formal establishment. Jenny was later to narrate a video on ovarian cancer, that won a British Medical Association bronze award and was available to view at the centre. In recognition of her vision and work to create the charity, a plaque in commemoration of Sarah was also displayed.

In parallel with the success of the "adopt a hospital" scheme, the level of invitations to Ovacome committee members and volunteers to attend exhibitions, conferences and seminars began to rise rapidly throughout 1998. As just one example, in the autumn, Louise Bayne and Ruth Payne manned an exhibition stand for Ovacome at a study day on ovarian cancer held at the Royal College of Obstetrics and Gynaecology, a prestigious event. This was quickly followed by a similar event in London, sponsored by Bristol-Myers Squibb (BMS), who by now had replaced SB as a main sponsor of Ovacome, founded on their paclitaxel treatment. Other London events followed.

But attendance at prestigious medical professional events was not the only type of exhibition that members put on and certainly London was not the sole focus of those events. In early 1999, Barbara Pike, a relatively new member of the charity and also the raising awareness co-ordinator for the North of England, met with two other local members, Heather Coyle and Margaret Borthwick, over lunch. They told her that each year the charity celebrated Sarah Dickinson's birthday (8th April) by holding an Ovacome Day and that members throughout the country were encouraged to hold events and, hopefully, raise awareness and funds. Barbara began to think about what they could do locally and, just as time was getting short, she took a telephone call from a young woman, Alison Herron, who told her the moving story of her mother's experience with and ultimate death from ovarian cancer. Alison and her two sisters, Gayle and Gillian, enthusiastically agreed the use of their mother's story to promote the charity on Ovacome Day, through a local exhibition.

Everyone sprang into action. The first decision was to exhibit at the most prominent site they could arrange at short notice and through a collaboration with Gateshead Health (now a NHS Foundation Trust) the management of the massive and iconic Metrocentre was approached. Happily, they agreed to provide a promotional space in the centre at no charge.

Barbara recognised that attracting media attention would be critical to their success and, again through Gateshead Health, she managed to arrange interviews for Gillian and herself with the local newspaper. A hilarious time was then had with the newspaper's photographer, joined by Alison and Gayle and, true to their word, the paper carried a half-page exclusive story with photographs in their Good Friday edition, providing massive local publicity just a few days before the event. Barbara also wanted a qualified medical professional to be there on the day to help answer questions and give advice and thankfully a specialist Macmillan Cancer Care nurse, Karen, volunteered.

The morning of the 8th April arrived and all was set. All the volunteers looking after the stand throughout the day and evening wore Ovacome T-shirts which made it easy for the public to identify them. Barbara had been anxious about how successful the day would be but she need not have worried; it was a stunning success. As the stand was being put up, before the shops had opened, people were coming over asking for information. Throughout much of the day there were queues at the stand with lots of questions asked of the volunteers and so many information leaflets and membership forms taken that further copies had to be hurriedly photocopied as supplies ran out within the first 90 minutes. Ultimately, and incredibly, around 500 leaflets and factsheets were given out on the day. During the afternoon all three sisters joined those at the stand and were able to relate the story of their mother to those who called by: a poignant time for each of them. Gateshead Health's press department arranged more media coverage as the BBC's Radio Newcastle station sent a reporter to interview ladies at the stand and local BBC TV ran features on the event both the evening before and throughout Ovacome Day itself. At 9pm, exhausted but very happy, the team dismantled the stand but even as they did, one more shopper came over to ask questions and gather information. Eleven hours had flown by. A tremendous success and a brilliant example of how a collaboration between a charity and a local health service can benefit both parties.

A few months after the Metrocentre success, Ruth Payne led Ovacome's presence at the largest exhibition for those involved in primary care: GPs, practice nurses, health visitors and other professionals. Ruth, a practice nurse herself, was well aware that knowledge of the disease amongst these professionals was not at a high enough level and wanted to take every opportunity to raise it. In 1999 the conference was held at the Birmingham National Exhibition Centre and spanned two days of events and presentations. Once again, Ovacome members put up a stand and staffed it throughout the conference. The main focus of the stand was to promote a quiz to establish how much attendees knew about ovarian cancer. Of over 500 entries to the quiz not a single person answered all the questions correctly, a quite frightening result. Through the exhibition, Ovacome managed to reach well over 1000 health care professionals and, hopefully, raised their awareness of the disease, particularly its symptoms and early impact.

Ovacome's heroines and heroes – Ruth Payne's story

Ruth became involved with Ovacome shortly after the charity's inception. In the spring of 1996, Ruth was 41 years old, living in London, married with two children and working as a qualified nurse. She read Sarah Dickinson's article in Good Housekeeping *magazine and decided to contact Sarah to offer her help which was gratefully accepted. What Ruth did not know at the time, but was to find out four months later, was that she too had developed ovarian cancer.*

Looking back on that time, Ruth recognises that the warning signs had been there for her to see but even as a qualified nurse she did not recognise them, or at least attribute them to anything serious. She had noticed some change in bowel habit and, for a short time, became quite tired and even depressed. But it took the strangest experience to prompt her to see her GP; she got stuck under the steering wheel of her car due to a bloated stomach.

Her GP's initial thought was that Ruth was pregnant, but this was soon dismissed and she was referred for a scan. As a nurse, Ruth understood the scan process well and recognised immediately that the radiologist was taking more time than usual to complete the process. The following morning another visit to her GP confirmed that the probable cause of her symptoms was ovarian cancer and she was referred to a gynaecological consultant. Unfortunately, it was three weeks before the consultation was held, diagnosis confirmed and a date for surgery set. During this period, Ruth became increasingly ill; more and more tired and bloated.

Once in hospital, there was a further scare when two doctors came to see her and had a small argument over which one of them was going to tell her that they had identified a problem with her liver. At this moment, Ruth thought that her future was bleak. Fortunately, the liver problem turned out to be nothing more than reaction to pressure being exerted by the ovarian tumour. Surgery went ahead the next day, removing a tumour that weighed 18 lbs (about 8 kilos), together with radical hysterectomy. There was some good news; no metastasis was found.

Following surgery, Ruth's oncologist wanted her to join the ICON 3 trial that was studying the impact on the disease of combining cisplatin or carboplatin with Taxol as opposed to either of the platinum-based drugs alone. Ruth considered this but decided, as her cancer was early stage, to proceed with carboplatin only, undergoing six cycles in the months that followed. Overall, it took six months for Ruth to recover from the fatigue brought on by the surgery and chemotherapy plus the many infections she contracted due to a weakened immune system. A few years later Ruth was tested for the mutated BRCA1 and 2 genes, but this proved to be negative – a relief for her.

Towards the end of her recovery period, Ruth became more active with Ovacome again and recalls attending the launch event that culminated in Alexandra Park Windsor in September 1996. Ruth became one of Ovacome's first Fone Friends, fielding calls from her home prior to the first office being opened. Through her work as a nurse and her own experience of the disease, Ruth was passionate about the need to improve awareness of symptoms with both the medical profession and the public and, with others, attended many events and conferences to "spread the word". The following year, Ruth joined the "raising awareness" task force (one of the four task forces established by the charity's committee) which at that time was led by Louise Bayne, a midwife and fellow committee member. In 1999, when Louise became chairperson of Ovacome, Ruth was the obvious choice to become the leader of the task force.

When Ovacome opened its first office in December 2000 Ruth joined the staff team and provided telephone-based support services to members. In later years, she helped with the administration of the charity in addition to her member support duties, finally becoming Ovacome's first support services nurse in early 2012, a role she kept until her retirement in the autumn of 2016. Even then she continued her involvement with the "younger women's" group of the charity.

Ruth was involved with the charity, either as volunteer or employee, for a twenty-year period. Over that time she saw many changes, including six office moves, as Ovacome went from strength to strength. She was part of the bedrock of the charity and is, to this day, a passionate supporter of its work.

Two further channels supported Ovacome's raising awareness objective during the latter part of the 1990s. The first was the creation of the charity's first website. Adrian Dickinson, Sarah's husband, took the lead on this project, recognising in those early days of the internet that a web presence would become a critical communication path to members. Work on the site was carried out through the summer of 1997 and it was launched in the autumn with, by today's standards, the ancient web address of http:dspace.dial.pipex.com/ovacome/. The site hosted a home page that provided basic introductory information; web copies of the newsletters; details of Fone Friends contacts; a description of the charity; a section outlining how people could get involved and contribute to the charity's aims and a "HelpFinder" facility that directed members and the broader public to other organisations and publications that they might find useful. For its time, the website was both innovative and comprehensive and was much acclaimed by the increasing numbers of members who had access to the internet. In later years it was to become the mainstay of the charity's connection to its members, especially so in 2020.

The second was (and still is) the newsletter itself. From the beginning, each newsletter carried at least one article written by a member describing their experience of the disease; the symptoms, the diagnosis, the treatment and the impact, both physical and psychological, on them, their family and their friends. All written in a candid and heartfelt way, these stories quickly became the bedrock of the newsletter for many members who related to and took comfort from the experiences of others.

But the newsletter developed rapidly to provide a wealth of information beyond those individual stories. From the second edition, published in the summer of 1996, articles describing research and new treatment possibilities appeared with both of the drugs topotecan and paclitaxel (Taxol) featuring in that year. Over the next three years, the newsletter covered (amongst many others) topics as diverse as:

- Financial advice for sufferers including information on the financial benefits available and where to go for further advice and support with money problems
- The part (or not) that talcum powder plays in the development of ovarian cancer
- The role and value of counselling
- Developments in clinical trials and screening for ovarian cancer
- The use of head scarves and wigs
- Sexuality and fertility with ovarian cancer

An important feature of the newsletter has always been to embrace a wide range of topics, viewpoints and writing styles, for example, through humour. Whilst humour in ovarian cancer is a rare luxury for most, one contributor begged to differ. Rachel Solemani was diagnosed in April 1997 and shortly after, she started to chronicle her experience in a very humorous monologue. Sadly, Rachel died in February 1999 but with the approval of her family, much of her monologue was published, some of it posthumously, in newsletters spanning 1998 to 2000 under the title "The Wicked Woman's Cancer". The honest and moving, as well as funny, articles included the following observations:

Rachel's initial diagnosis and treatment:

"April fool's day 1997. Coming from a family of practical jokers I had to endure some pretty tough ones in my time. But this one! I am in the gynae ward of my local hospital, whisked into an unknown world of major scans and blood tests. A world of cancer. There are large suspect masses on my ovaries. It was as if life had played its cruellest joke on me and no one is going to shout those comforting words - April fool, only joking."

"Had I noticed any symptoms? At Christmas when I was about to buy a "little black number" that I had promised myself for years, the short beautiful beaded dress I had set my heart on made me look like an overstuffed Christmas turkey. Then, when I was making a hurried exit from my daughter's Christmas concert to avoid being accosted by evangelicals from the Parent Staff Association to sell Christmas cards, I was stopped in my tracks by a women I scarcely knew. 'When is your baby due?' she asked. I made a thinly disguised effort to hide my horror and rushed out to M&S to by a stomach reducer or minimiser as it is euphemistically called."

"Three days later I am waking up in the recovery room after major surgery. I have become a screaming wild woman, yelling at anyone and everyone to tell me what they have found. I know I have cancer because no one has told me I haven't. Yes, it is cancer with tumours as big as an orange and a grapefruit my surgeon tells me the next day (no wonder I needed the stomach reducer)."

"My elder daughter comes to see me on her way back from school. I am delighted to see her despite all of the tubes sticking out of me. 'Oh, you don't look as bad as I thought you would,' she says. 'Hair's a bit of a mess though.' Sorry, I retort, I couldn't get to the hairdressers with my new fashion accessories – the drips and the stomach drain."

"So, what am I to do? Nothing like a serious illness to bring out the bitch in me. Devil women is emerging. This wicked woman has to carry on."

"I am back home ... learning about cancer at a speed that would make the average medical student sweat. Browsing, or frantically flicking, through medical textbooks I find out what ovaries are: 'Ovary, one pair of almond shaped glands.' I have cancer because something went wrong with my almonds?"

"Time for the oncologist! Mr Non Committal. With the medical texts fresh in my mind, I ask him about the stage of the cancer. If you ask, no punches are pulled. Stage 4. The cancer has seeded, what they call metastasised in the bleak world of cancer jargon. I've well and truly got the "mets" and that means heavy duty chemotherapy for you, lady!"

"Back to the waiting room. I am given a booklet, *Diet and the Cancer Patient*. Inwardly I rage; I am being reduced to a cancer patient. Can you be a glamorous cancer patient? How do cancer patients behave? In the case of this one, badly, I hope. After playing spot-who's-wearing-the-wig for a few minutes, I chat with a friendly lady wearing a brightly coloured scarf. She's got cancer too. Well of course she has or she wouldn't be here. 'It's all in the mind,' she tells me. I resist helping her along to a quick and violent death. Do they give you chemotherapy in Holloway prison? It's about controlling your impulses to become a serial killer of all those people who tell you ever so nicely that you've got to let go of your anger and eat up your vegetables."

Rachel was not a great believer in alternative or complementary remedies or therapies as the following passages demonstrated:

"Today I was sent a bunch of pamphlets of the 'alternative' medicine variety. Those who do not advise you to reject conventional treatment, prefer the term 'complementary'. I pick up a leaflet on *Keeping Hope Alive*. Well, I certainly need that after reading the text: 'Essiac tea is said to have cured thousands of terminal cancer cases since the 1920s.' One was a women with guess what? An ovarian tumour 'as big as a grapefruit' who was cured by the tea drinking. Amazing! All I have to do is drink tea!"

"I read on. Other pamphlets by American doctors: the Dr Quacks and Dr Frauds... Not medical doctors. According to Dr Fraud and his buddy, Dr Quack, Echinacea cures AIDs and cancer. Oh and by the way, so does garlic. By that account I should be cured of cancer by now, or I shouldn't have it in the first place, with the amount of garlic I've consumed in my life."

"Last week some well-meaning soul passed me an article about some Italian research claiming to demonstrate that fatalities from ovarian cancer increased in direct proportion to the number of fried eggs the woman ate. The fewer fried eggs, the fewer fatalities. Simple really. I must tell my consultant not to bother with all these expensive trials costing millions of pounds or these scans that cost thousands to operate or these incredibly costly drugs – just tell the woman not to eat fried eggs."

"This is my day for the alternative, sorry, complementary cancer centre. Everyone is terribly nice. I have an aromatherapy massage and try a 'bit of healing' with an ageing hippy type with a wispy beard... He moves his hands a few inches from my body, sort of outlining it. He doesn't say a lot but says he can feel a lot of energy. I confirm that I am a very energetic person."

"We go back into a room and they ask me if I want to join a meditation. I read in the pamphlet on the way home that many people with cancer find it 'empowering' to go on a raw diet and practice meditating and healing. Maybe they do. But it's not really my idea of a rave up. Give me a good party any day."

"The next day my 'Learning to Meditate' package arrives. Gosh, it's hard work being a cancer patient! After sitting in my 'suitably darkened' room, practising my mantra and getting irritated by the supposedly 'calming' voice I decide I've had enough. Cancer or no cancer, the life of a nun is not for me. Give me glamour! Bond Street here I come."

Rachel on the subject of friends and their reactions to her illness:

"I feel I could write a book on what not to say to a person who has cancer. For example don't say 'when my auntie was dying of breast cancer we...' Chances are that their auntie was at least 30 years older than me and grandmothers to boot."

"'Be brave' they say – do they know how irritating that is? What do they know about it, they haven't got cancer! Why should I be brave anyway, if I don't want to? This is all the 'battling' with cancer mentality that is bandied about. Is 'fighting' the disease putting up with chemo? Do they think those who die haven't done this?"

"Some friends desert you all together. They simply cannot handle the whole thing. Then there are some who don't desert you but you wish they had. Unconsciously they think you are going to contaminate them or magically transmit the disease to them. God help those who do have a transmissible illness!"

"Some folks think you have done something wrong. You can see that they think that if only you had taken Chinese herbs or been a vegetarian you wouldn't have cancer. They say how weird it is that Linda McCartney should have died of cancer."

"Yes, it is a no-win situation, there isn't a right or wrong thing to say to the person with cancer – there is no instruction booklet. That is until I write my very own: 'damn you if you are not interested and damn you if you are'. I suppose I can say all this because, at the end of the day, I have got some brilliant friends who stick with me through it all when I am a difficult bitch. You can even forgive them for their constant gynaecological check-ups. Of course they don't want to end up like 'everyone's worst nightmare', in other words... yours truly."

As if to balance Rachel's possibly tongue-in-cheek comments on alternative or complementary remedies and treatments, the newsletter provided a platform for a very strong advocate of such measures, Diane Chapman. From the spring of 1997, Diane's 'With Complements' articles featured regularly up to the point of her sad passing in February 2001.

Diane had been diagnosed with ovarian cancer in December 1994 and underwent surgery, several cycles of chemotherapy and a stem cell transplant. She became a member of Ovacome shortly after it was formed and was soon an active Fone Friend, later becoming one of the first Fone Friends task force members and a member of the charity's committee. Being a person of determination and energy, shortly after her diagnosis, Diane began to research the value of diet, complementary treatments and remedies and this became an abiding passion and driving force for her over the next six years.

From the outset, Diane was clear that complementary remedies would not cure cancer. However, she believed passionately that they could help alongside conventional treatments, to keep the disease at bay and hence prolong remission and quality of life.

Her early comments spoke of the positive impact a very healthy diet could have. She championed eating fruit, unprocessed whole foods, less meat and more vegetables (raw when possible), less dairy product and eggs and the consumption of green and/or herbal tea. In the 2020s, much of this advice has become relatively mainstream but in 1997/8 it was less common, even cutting-edge.

Next she moved on to the subject of nutritional supplements such as vitamins and minerals. She outlined the effect of each supplement and explained, in clear language, how they could help with cancer treatment. Diane was always careful to present a balanced view of the pros and cons of each and provided comprehensive information, allowing the reader to assess and make up their own mind as to what would be best for them.

Exercise was another topic that received Diane's attention. Once again, she was measured in her advice, making it clear that heading to the gym for a vigorous workout shortly after surgery was not a good idea! Instead, she recommended gentle walking, gradually increasing the length and pace of walks as strength returned. If even walking was too much effort, she described the benefits of brushing the skin which helped to stimulate circulation and lymphatic drainage. Finally, she recommended water therapy which consisted of standing under the shower with the water as hot as was bearable for 15 seconds, followed by water as cold as could be tolerated for 15 seconds and then repeating the process for 15 minutes, followed by a loud scream to fill the lungs with oxygen. Diane realised that for many, maybe most, this was a daunting prospect, but she believed strongly that the benefits were worth the pain. A little later, in the autumn of 1998, Diane wrote of the positive impact that relaxation and meditation could have on the progression of ovarian cancer.

Towards the end of 1997, Diane's CA-125 level began to rise and eventually her consultant recommended a further course of chemotherapy, this time with the drug topotecan. Diane was not convinced that more chemotherapy was the best way forward at that point and took a decision to take a more radical approach to her complementary therapy. The first enactment of that decision was to embark on the Gerson diet.

The Gerson diet was quite rigorous, even extreme, and included "super feeding" with organic vegetables and fruit, along with a daily intake of 13 freshly pressed vegetable and fruit juices packed with live enzymes. More radical still and at least a little controversial was the inclusion of coffee enemas (as Diane wrote: "yes, I did say coffee enemas"). Although after following the diet meticulously over many months, Diane's cancer did not subside, and her abdomen began to fill with ascites. As a result, in the spring of 1998, she moved on to the next, even more radical (for that time) treatment regime known as hyperthermia. For this she booked into a clinic in Germany for an initial two-week period. During this time her ascites was drained and she received small infusions of cisplatin directly into her abdomen. This was accompanied with heat treatment (hyperthermia) to her abdomen. Over the two-week period, Diane underwent six similar treatments, although cisplatin was infused on only two of those occasions. Diane returned to the clinic for two further, one week, stays to have the same treatment and then took a two-week course of cyclophosphamide tablets at home. During her final week at the clinic, scans taken revealed no tumours and her CA-125 level had fallen but not back into the normal range. Diane firmly believed that the Gerson diet and her treatment in Germany had resulted in a dramatic reduction in her cancer although she recognised that it might not have the positive effect on others that she had experienced.

Not surprisingly, her view was at least a little controversial. In the newsletter that followed publication of Diane's article, Doctor Richard Osborne, then a medical oncologist at Poole Cancer Centre, Dorset, set out, in balanced terms, his personal views on Gerson, hyperthermia and intraperitoneal (the infusion of drugs directly into the abdominal cavity) chemotherapy. Clearly, he was a little more sceptical than Diane of the relative benefits of those treatments. As always, Ovacome was keen to provide an open forum for discussion of this topic and several further articles, some more and some less supportive of Diane's views, were published.

Over the next two years, Diane continued to write regular articles for Ovacome's newsletter covering topics that included: the use of Essiac, a herbal treatment made up of four herbs (sheep sorrel, burdock root, slippery elm and Turkey rhubarb root) pioneered by a Canadian lady, Rene Caisse (Essiac is Caisse spelt backwards) in the 1930s; hydrazine sulphate, a compound also used in rocket fuel introduced by Dr Joseph Gold of the Syracuse Institute in the 1960s and claimed to halt tumour growth; the use of certain vaccines to stimulate the immune system to attack cancer; the discovery of inositol hexaphosphate (IP6), championed by Dr Abulkalam Shamsuddin at the University of Maryland's school of medicine in the USA, a supplement which claimed to help cancer cells to become more like normal cells; finally, the role of minute quantities of cyanide, attached to an antibody, in killing cancer cells. Throughout all of these later articles, Diane was, once again, meticulous in giving a balanced view of each of the complementary treatments she wrote about.

Over a four-year period, Diane had used Ovacome's newsletter to communicate her findings, often based on considerable research, for the knowledge and potential benefit of fellow sufferers. In addition to her articles, Diane also wrote and published a book, titled *With*

Complements in 1997. An important contribution to the debate on the treatment of ovarian cancer.

As the 1990s came to a close, Ovacome's newsletter had transformed from a few pages largely consisting of individual stories plus some treatment news to a fully-fledged, highly informative, often entertaining quarterly journal much loved by members, as proven through membership surveys and the many members' letters published each quarter. By the latter part of the 1990s, well recognised and regarded medical professionals were contributing to the newsletter, providing both opinion pieces and expert articles. Doctor Ian Jacobs, a senior oncologist at St Bartholomew's in London, who had been involved at the launch of Ovacome, was amongst these professionals and soon joined the charity's committee, becoming the charity's first medical advisor. A specialist gynaecological cancer nurse, Karen Summerville, became a regular contributor covering a wide range of topics related to ovarian cancer. But most importantly, the newsletter was still rooted in the founding principles of the charity. It was still the members' newsletter; their stories at the heart, and their needs guiding its content.

The charity itself had evolved radically over a three year period from one women's – Sarah Dickinson – vision into an important driving force in the support of ovarian cancer sufferers and their families and friends. Well respected, sought out by medical professionals and government officials for information and comment, loved and owned by its membership, which, at the end of 1999, stood at well over 1000.

ROBERT LEACH

As the bells of Big Ben chimed midnight on the 31st December 1999 and fireworks lit up the sky from the newly installed millennium wheel overlooking the River Thames, plus many other locations across the country, Ovacome had achieved so much more than Sarah and her group of "kitchen table" friends could have imagined. And as the clocks moved on to one minute past midnight, the new millennium and the opportunities and challenges for Ovacome began.

Chapter 3

GROWING PAINS, TRIALS
AND TRIBULATIONS

Growing pains

As the 20th century came to a close, Ovacome had come a long way. But in common with many start-up organisations that grow rapidly, Ovacome was experiencing some growing pains. In late 1999, the charity had appointed a new chairperson, Louise Bayne. Louise, a midwife, had been involved with the charity for two years, first as a Fone Friend and later as the raising awareness co-ordinator and took the chair at a time of change for the charity as it began the next stage of its development.

The first challenge was to improve the infrastructure of Ovacome to put it on a more sustainable footing for the future. This required some fundamental decisions to be taken as, up to that point, the charity had been run entirely by volunteers, all working from home using their personal space, telephones and, sometimes, computers. This had to change if Ovacome was to thrive in the newly dawned 21st century. Realising this, the charity's committee agreed to employ staff for the first time and to find an office for them to work from. Volunteers Alex Whates and Debbie Howells became Ovacome's first part-time employees, recruited to help with management and administration. Quite quickly a trained counsellor, Frances Hodges, was added to the staff team. Frances had been a member of the charity's committee and had been providing voluntary telephone counselling for members, their family and friends, from her home since the spring. Frances was joined by Ruth Payne, a qualified nurse and together they were able to provide office-based telephone counselling support to members from 9am to 5pm each workday, the first time this had been possible. This support was in addition and complementary to the Fone Friends network, which continued its highly valuable work. As the year 2000 progressed and membership continued to increase, further part-time staff were employed, and the team began to take shape.

The search for premises commenced in the summer of 2000 and was concluded later that year when an office was opened in St Bartholomew's (Bart's) hospital on December 3rd. As Ruth Payne recalls, this "office" was little more than a corner of a laboratory but at least it was a home for the charity and its staff. About eighteen months later, the team relocated to a basement office in Bart's next door to that of a group of scientific staff working on a major ovarian cancer clinical trial of the time: the UK Collaborative Trial of Ovarian Cancer Screening (UKCTOCS). This office served well for a year or so but was not ideal and in the autumn of 2003 the staff team moved into new and more suitable premises at the Elizabeth Garrett Anderson hospital in London.

Ovacome was, finally, established in an office that fully met its needs, at least for a few years.

In summer 2003, a decision was taken to create a new role, that of director of the charity. Louise Bayne was asked to take this role, which was the senior operating management position, and readily accepted. A new chairperson, Rosemarie Williams, who had been a member of the charity's committee for a year, was appointed. The goal of these changes was to separate the governance role of chairperson from the operating role of director and to provide even more focus for both.

In other exciting developments, in the second half of 2003 a project was launched to develop a brand new website. The original site had been set up in 1999, one of the first for a charity but web technology had raced ahead, and the site had become outdated and needed replacement. The new site was to offer new functionality, including up-to-date news of interest, online access to newsletters, merchandising capability and a chat room.

Whilst staff roles, premises, organisation structure and technology were being improved, other actions to advance Ovacome's reach, authority and impact were being planned and implemented. One crucial initiative was to establish, in 2000, a medical advisory board, the first such body within an ovarian cancer charity in the UK. Ovacome was fortunate enough to be able to appoint, as the first director of that board, Ian Jacobs, then professor of gynaecological oncology at St Mary's University, London, and a very good friend of the charity.

Ovacome's heroines and heroes – Professor Ian Jacobs

Ian Jacobs was born in the East End of London and raised in North London where his parents ran a retail pharmacy. He was the first of his family to attend university, taking bachelor and master's degrees in medicine and law at Trinity College Cambridge. He then trained further and qualified as a doctor at Middlesex Hospital Medical School in 1983. The following year he began specialist training in obstetrics and gynaecology, initially at the Royal London Hospital and then at Addenbrooke's Hospital, Cambridge, which he completed in 1990. From that point on, Ian became very involved in medical research focusing increasingly on gynaecological cancers, particularly ovarian cancer, working initially at Bart's and The Royal Marsden Hospital, and then at Queen Mary University, London, and University College London.

Subsequently, his medical and academic career took him from London to Manchester (2011), where he was dean of the faculty of medicine at Manchester University and then to Sydney, Australia (2015) as president and vice chancellor of the University of New South Wales. In January 2021, he announced his intention to step down from that role and to return to the UK in January 2022. Over his career, Ian has been involved in many research programmes but possibly the most prominent was his launch and overall leadership of the "United Kingdom Collaborative Trial of Ovarian Cancer Screening" (UKCTOCS) programme, which ran for 35 years in total.

Whilst working as a junior doctor in 1985, Ian became very concerned at the high incidence of death in those diagnosed with ovarian cancer. This early experience led him to devise the UKCTOCS programme to establish if a screening methodology could reliably identify ovarian cancer at an early stage, paving the way for immediate treatment that would save lives. The programme was based on two screening methods, the monitoring of CA-125 levels in the blood and ultrasound scanning.

Over the first 15 years, working with colleagues in the UK and the USA, the screening techniques were refined and a "risk of ovarian cancer algorithm" developed. During those 15 years, over 50,000 patients were involved in the trial and the results at that point in time were promising, indicating that the screening process devised did detect ovarian cancer at earlier stages in 85% of cases.

In 2000, the programme was extended and over the next 20 years approximately 200,000 patients were involved in the study. Once again, the initial results were promising and confirmed the 85% early detection ratio as seen in the initial work. But the big question still to be answered was whether the screening approach reduced mortality or not. By 2015, preliminary data on mortality suggested that it did but the results were not definitive. The researchers were tantalisingly close to a major breakthrough in reducing ovarian cancer deaths. Five years later, in May 2021, the final results were published and reviewed. To everyone's huge disappointment, even despair, they demonstrated no significant reduction in deaths from ovarian cancer. The screening process did bring forward the time of diagnosis but did not improve overall survival. As Ian noted in an article he authored regarding the conclusions, he and his colleagues were devastated and sad. The search for a reliable, safe and affordable screening programme for ovarian cancer continues.

Ian became involved with Ovacome at its inception, whilst he was a registrar in gynaecology at Bart's. He had been one of two senior oncologists to speak at the launch event in 1996, Professor Martin Gore of the Royal Marsden hospital being the other. Ian had been very supportive of the charity in helping find its first offices at Bart's, the hospital from which he ran the UKCTOC's clinical trial. On joining the charity's committee in 1997 he became Ovacome's first medical advisor and began to contribute articles to the newsletter from the autumn of that year, covering many medical issues related to ovarian cancer.

Ian was not a newcomer to charities. In 1984, recently qualified, he had launched the forerunner of the Eve Appeal, then named the Gynaecology Cancer Research Fund. The charity focused on raising funds for research into ovarian cancer, although in later years it widened its focus to include all five gynaecological cancers. In the years ahead, Ovacome and the Eve Appeal would work together on several different initiatives and programmes and even share an office for a short time.

By 2000, Ian had been contributing to Ovacome for more than three years and he was the obvious choice to lead the highly distinguished medical advisory board established in the summer of that year. The board consisted of 25 medical professionals from around the country, representing many disciplines relevant to ovarian cancer. The terms of reference for the board were set out clearly:

- Preparing articles for the Ovacome newsletter
- Preparing responses to frequently asked questions received by Ovacome
- Reviewing the Ovacome newsletter.

The overall objective was to assist the charity's committee and its members by providing specialist expertise and advice but not to be involved with editorial decisions which remained firmly with the charity's management.

Ian continued to actively support Ovacome and lead the medical advisory board until 2003 when work pressures required him to step down. He had played a pivotal role in ensuring that the charity was always up to date with latest developments in research, diagnosis and treatment and ensuring that the charity reported accurate and relevant information to members and the broader public. Through his efforts and that of the Medical Advisory Board as a whole, the authority of Ovacome in the world of ovarian cancer was significantly enhanced.

Ovacome's international presence and reach took a big step forward in the summer of 2001 when Louise Bayne, the charity's director, was invited to a conference, sponsored by Astra Zeneca, a leading pharmaceutical company, and held in New York. Leaders of many national ovarian cancer charities attended, and Louise remembers being enthused by sharing knowledge and experiences with others facing the same challenges and opportunities as Ovacome. One important outcome of the conference was the setting up of an international ovarian cancer forum with the aim of continuing the sharing and mutual support that had been so rewarding in New York.

From inception, member engagement had been a big focus for Ovacome. Starting with the publication of letters written by members and continuing through the Fone Friends network and other voluntary work. However, the charity's committee felt that member engagement needed to be taken further and implemented several initiatives to that effect. First, in the spring of 2003, the "members' weekend", was introduced. On the first morning of the inaugural event, attendees listened to presentations from several doctors, covering many aspects of ovarian cancer treatments and were updated on the results of the recently completed ICON 4 clinical trial. The afternoon focused more on the work of the charity and its future plans, inviting comment and suggestions for improvement; these were taken forward into the first strategy day being held by the charity's committee a couple of months later. The following day was devoted to counselling techniques and the Fone Friends network with a lively discussion of how that could be improved. Again, those suggestions were later input to the committee's strategy day.

Everyone agreed that the event had been a huge success. Members attending had been given insights into latest medical thinking and initiatives and had been given the opportunity to input into the future direction and plans of the charity. But the greatest value had come from the discussion groups and informal chats over coffee, tea and dinner that had created many bonds, both between members, new and old, and with staff. The members' weekend was to become a regular event in the years ahead.

Second, in October, the newsletter gained a new editor, Jayne Piper, and an editorial board was set up. Members were surveyed to seek their views of the newsletter and to put forward ideas for its improvement. Their comments helped to shape both the format and content of the publication in the months and years ahead.

Finally, in what had been a very busy year, 2003 closed with the launch of a major new initiative: the introduction of regional Ovacome co-ordinators (ROCs). ROCs partly replaced the Fone Friends scheme which had been running successfully for the past seven years but needed refreshing. The demands on and opportunities for the charity to be more engaged with local authorities, medical professionals, other related charities or organisations and the media had grown significantly over the past two to three years and the charity's committee was determined to meet this need. ROCs had a considerably broader remit than the previous Fone Friends co-ordinators and focused on a smaller area, usually a county. In many respects they were the "face" of the charity in their area. At the outset the role was defined as:

- To be a point of contact for people wishing to talk to others in their area
- To attend occasional fundraising events on behalf of the charity

- To co-ordinate local volunteers, enabling them to distribute Ovacome material to local hospitals and other sites
- To hold details of local members wishing to talk to the media
- To hold occasional get-togethers for local members if appropriate

In the space of a few years Ovacome had transformed its structure, representation and output making it clearer, more authoritative and professional. A highly respected voice for ovarian cancer sufferers throughout the country.

Trials

Clinical trials had long been a feature of the research effort into potential new treatments for ovarian cancer and was to become a sustained focus of information dissemination by the charity. Within a few weeks of formation, Ovacome began highlighting these trials, reporting on both the Imperial Cancer Research Funds trials of monoclonal antibodies and SmithKline Beecham's trials of Hycamtin (topotecan) in the summer of 1996. Two years later the newsletter carried an article that explained briefly several important ongoing and planned trials of the time: International Collaborative Ovarian Neoplasm (ICON) 1, 3 and 4, plus OVA 5 and 6. These were international trials that tested several different drugs and drug combinations for use against initial, advanced or recurrent disease.

Trials and the debate around them progressed to a new level in 2002/3 with publication of the results of the ICON 3 trial which proved to be at least partly controversial. ICON 3 had enrolled over 2000 participants internationally to establish the benefits of combining the platinum-based drug, carboplatin, with paclitaxel compared to carboplatin or cisplatin alone, in first line therapy. Both the set-up of the trial and the interpretation of the results, particularly when compared to other contemporary trials involving paclitaxel, drew considerable comment from many oncologists. Despite the controversy, Ovacome was determined to report the findings and conclusions in an even-handed manner and to provide balanced advice to its members. As such, between late 2002 and mid-2003, the conflicting views of medical professionals on the results and conclusions of the trial were published in the newsletters of the time. Later in 2003, the charity reported that the National Institute of Clinical Excellence (NICE), which up to that point had recommended paclitaxel/platinum drug combination therapy, had changed its position. Founded partly on the ICON 3 results, NICE recommended giving patients the choice of undergoing either combination or platinum drug therapy alone, following discussions with their consultant.

Hot on the heels of ICON 3 came the ICON 4 trial that was similar to ICON 3 but focused on patients who had been treated successfully and then relapsed after six months or more. Once again, reported by Ovacome, the results of this trial were less controversial and supported the benefits of combination therapy over platinum drug alone regimes.

By the middle of the 2000s, Ovacome had provided much needed data and information to members regarding the various trials of treatments; information that had been difficult to access in the past, at least for the lay person. Up to that point, most of the trials reported had commenced prior to Ovacome's establishment. That was to change in the years ahead as the charity took on more of a role in publicising and promoting novel treatment trials in addition to reporting the results.

Tribulations

Virtually all young charities face a common challenge, that of raising sufficient funds to keep up with the demands on its resources and to sustain growth. Ovacome was no different. From the very beginning, the charity had relied on the goodwill of early committee members to launch Ovacome and soon thereafter many members began to contribute through a variety of individual fundraising events, activities and direct donations. From 1997 onwards, Ovacome Christmas cards were designed, printed and sold; coffee mornings and tea parties were held in members' homes; members embarked on sponsored walks, runs (including the London and other marathons), bicycle rides and hill climbs, including a "three peaks challenge" completed by Ovacome supporter, Christine Johnson. The challenge required Christine, together with eleven other brave souls, to climb to the top of Ben Nevis, Scafell Pike and Mount Snowdon within the space of 24 hours. Although the weather was poor, with rain much of the time, the group commenced the climb of Ben Nevis at 6:30pm, walking through snow close to the summit. After descending they boarded their minibus and grabbed a few hours' sleep as they were driven to Scafell arriving by 5am. The climb up Scafell and back started immediately and by 10am they were back in the minibus heading to Wales and Mount Snowdon, arriving at 3pm. Time was now quite short as the group had to reach the summit of Snowdon by 6pm to have successfully met the challenge. The climb was difficult with very slippery conditions underfoot but with some good fortune and a lot of determination, the summit was achieved with about an hour to spare. Exhausted but happy, the group took photographs of each other on the peak and then started the slow descent.

Christine's mother had died of ovarian cancer in 1993 and was the inspiration for her to take on the challenge. Through her commitment and courage, she had raised personally several hundred pounds for the charity. As Louise Bayne, director of the charity, stated at the time: "Everyone at Ovacome is in awe of you". A well-deserved tribute.

Whilst Christine's memorable climb and many of the hundreds of other wonderful events that took place around the country were "one-offs", other fundraising events became annual fixtures in the Ovacome calendar. For several years, one such was the Flora Light Challenge for Women. First introduced in 1998 and sponsored by Flora margarine, the challenge was a five-kilometre run or walk around a course in Hyde Park, London. By 2000, the first time that Ovacome suggested that members take part and raise sponsorship funds, the event had grown exponentially and thousands of individuals from across the country entered. In 2002, Ovacome had 20 participants in the event, all wearing stand-out Ovacome T-shirts for easy recognition amongst the crowds. By 2005, the event, now sponsored by Hydro

Active, a sports drink manufacturer, had become so popular that three venues hosted the "fun run" in London, Birmingham and Liverpool. Fun runs, marathons and similar events became an important means of fundraising for the charity.

Possibly the pinnacle of fundraising efforts during the early years of the charity's existence was the "Ovacome Day". First held in September 1997 and initially titled "The Annual Fund Raising Day", the goal was to promote awareness of ovarian cancer, as well as to raise funds for Ovacome, through members and supporters holding a broad range of sponsored events across the country. The day was a great success on both counts, firmly establishing the idea as a fixture on the Ovacome calendar. By 1999, the date had been moved to the 8th April each year to coincide with Sarah Dickinson's birthday and had been retitled Ovacome Day. One year later, the planning for the day had taken a big step forward with press releases being prepared for members' use and fundraising factsheets – full of great ideas and suggestions – being made available. Regional sponsored bicycle events were arranged across the country in addition to many less strenuous activities and when the day was over, thousands of pounds had been raised for the charity. Over the next four years, the Ovacome Day continued to provide much needed funds for the charity, with an ever increasing range of innovative activities.

All these voluntary, sometimes heroic, efforts put much needed funds into Ovacome's bank account, but they were prone to be sporadic, leading to difficulty in forecasting when and how much cash might arrive at any point in time. With a growing charity that, by the early 2000s, employed several staff; this became an increasing challenge. The year 2002 proved to be particularly difficult as the official mourning period for the Queen Mother, who had died on the 30th March that year, resulted in the cancellation, or at least curtailment, of many of the planned Ovacome Day activities, including a big event in London. The impact on cash receipts was significant and for the first time, the charity recorded a financial deficit in that year.

Louise Bayne recalls many committee meetings of the charity in the mid-2000s where the issue of fundraising, and how to improve both the quantum and predictability of cash receipts, was discussed. Employing a member of staff to focus on that specific challenge was considered at the time but the many calls on Ovacome's time and resources meant that it would be a further ten years before such an appointment was made.

Chapter 4

PICTURES PAINT A
THOUSAND WORDS

Raising awareness of ovarian cancer and providing support was, is and always will be Ovacome's raison d'être. Within three years of set-up, the charity had made real progress in achieving this goal, through information leaflets, conference attendance, local activities and media interviews. But much remained to be done and the charity's committee was always looking for new opportunities to spread the word.

Step forward a modest but determined young man with an idea, a cause and a passion. The young man was Andy Scaysbrook and the idea was to hold a photographic exhibition of celebrity personalities to gain publicity for the charity and its work; in fact, one exhibition turned into two exhibitions... Twelve years apart.

Ovacome's heroines and heroes – Andy Scaysbrook's (and his mum's) story

Andy Scaysbrook never planned to become a professional photographer. Like so much in life, it happened by chance, with a little push from his mum. On leaving school, Andy thought that he would be best suited to a career in the engineering industry and joined a local company in his native Coventry. Unfortunately, he was made redundant a few months later, joined another engineering company, was made redundant, joined another and was made redundant again.

Feeling a little disillusioned with engineering, Andy visited his local Job Centre to look for alternative ways of making a living and noticed a vacancy advertisement for a photographic assistant with a large commercial photography firm. He duly applied and was invited to an interview at which he was told that a decision would be made within the next day or two and that he would hear the result quite quickly. After one week had gone by Andy resigned himself to not getting the role but his mum kept urging him to telephone the firm and at least get a confirmation that he had not been successful. Eventually, and as Andy continued to show reluctance to make contact, his mum took the initiative and called the firm herself only to be told that he had been successful, that a letter confirming his appointment should have been posted to him and that he was due to start the very next day. Andy Scaysbrook's fledgling photographic career was launched.

For the next three years Andy supported the firm's team of photographers whilst at the same time attending college to study photography, portraiture in particular. The college programme inspired his creative instincts and, on realising that he would have to wait some time for a full photographer position to become available at his current firm, he took the bold decision to go freelance, initially working for a Midlands-based cricket magazine that often forgot to pay him. A useful early lesson in managing his own business.

One year later he was living in Bournemouth with his new girlfriend and working as a technician in a photographic laboratory and then for a local newspaper whilst continuing his freelance career. Then, somewhat to his surprise, he won a photographic award for some of his freelance work and the newspaper he worked for offered him the role of staff photographer. Andy held that role for the next seven years and then moved to Southampton to take up the position of picture editor for the Southampton Echo.

It was towards the end of his time in Bournemouth, 1997, that personal tragedy struck when his mum, Margaret, developed ovarian cancer. Andy's mum had been a nurse in her earlier life, working mostly in care homes but by the mid-1990s she and her husband were running a pub in Leicestershire, a busy occupation that demanded many hours of work at all times of the day. Margaret's experience with the symptoms of the disease and its diagnosis trod a similar path to that of many others. Noticing that her stomach was bloated she went to see her GP and was assured that there was nothing serious to worry about. As the symptoms worsened, more trips were made to doctors, with a similar outcome. Andy recalls visiting his mum and thinking that she "looked pregnant" but, typically, she played it down and told him not to worry. Eventually she was seen by a consultant at a hospital in Coventry where it was confirmed that she had advanced and inoperable ovarian cancer. *Given her nursing background and the advanced nature of the disease, Margaret decided not to undergo chemotherapy, or any other form of treatment but to enjoy as best she could the few months she had left to live. That is exactly what she did, visiting her son in Dorset and spending good times with him. Within six months of diagnosis, she had succumbed to the disease at the age of 57.*

Following his mum's death Andy continued his work at the Southampton Echo, *but the call of running his own business grew louder and some years later, in 2005, he left the embrace of employment for the second time and, once again, launched out on his own.*

Andy's re-entry to the world of photographic freelancing was a great success. Over the next 15 years or so he photographed many iconic figures including Pavarotti, Boris Johnson and Dame Ellen MacArthur. He also captured on film and catalogued several important and often moving events and experiences, for example, the plight of homeless people in Bristol, a Rolling Stones concert, a social documentary featuring the people of Cuba and, most recently, a moving depiction of front line health workers during the Covid crisis of 2020/21 titled 'Unmasked' which was featured in The Times *and* Sunday Times.

Andy has been and continues to be a great supporter of Ovacome, contributing his time, talent and passion to the charity across the years.

Whilst at the *Southampton Echo*, in the second half of 1999, Andy was asked to photograph a footballer called

David Howells who had been transferred from Tottenham Hotspur to Southampton the previous year. During the assignment, Andy was chatting with David and told him of his mum's recent death from ovarian cancer. This prompted David to mention that his wife, Debbie Howells, who had had ovarian cancer, worked with a relatively new charity, named Ovacome, that supported individuals affected by ovarian cancer. Around the same time, Andy attended an Ovacome members' day which he found emotionally difficult but informative and comforting at the same time. He became determined to do something to support Ovacome and shortly after his discussion with David Howells, he called Debbie to talk through an idea he had been mulling over for some weeks. That idea was to put on an exhibition of portraits of women celebrities to gain publicity for Ovacome and help raise awareness of the disease. Debbie was enthusiastic and following some discussion with the charity's management, Andy and Debbie began to collate a list of celebrities who would be approached and asked to agree to be photographed on behalf of the charity.

Over the next year, Andy and, sometimes, Debbie spoke with 35 possible candidates for the exhibition and ultimately 12 very well-known celebrities agreed to be involved: Jenny Agutter (patron of the charity), Jane Asher, Cherie Blair, Honor Bliss, Betty Boothroyd, Judy Finnigan, Fiona Fullerton, Sue Jenkins, Melinda Messenger, Carol Smillie, Anthea Turner and Jo Whiley. Andy travelled to each of these wonderful celebrities' homes to take the shots. He recalls, "all of the celebrities I photographed were welcoming, gracious and keen to help. When I arrived at Jane Asher's home in London, I was dumbstruck when her husband, the well-known illustrator and cartoonist, Gerald Scarfe, opened the front door. I am a great fan of Gerald's, and it was a pleasure to meet him as well as his wife. Photographing Cherie Blair in Downing Street was also an occasion to be remembered and, as a bit of a guitarist myself, I recall seeing Tony Blair's acoustic guitar hanging on the wall."

By the end of 2000, the photographs had all been taken and were ready for the exhibition. This was to be held at the St Jame's Club in Piccadilly, London, in the evening of April 6th 2001, effectively launching the charity's annual Ovacome Day celebration, which was to be held two days later. The exhibition was titled 'The Other Side of Me' and for Andy, personally, the evening was rather tense, not only because of the memories created of his mum but also that his wife was due to give birth to their first child that very day! Fortunately, that happy event was not to occur until two weeks later when a healthy son entered the world.

The exhibition was a great success and created, for a small charity at the time, massive media interest. Louise Bayne, the charity's chairperson at the time, described the event thus: "...this year's Ovacome Day events centred on a photographic exhibition by Andy Scaysbrook. Andy, whose mum sadly died of ovarian cancer, wanted to help raise the profile of the disease by staging an exhibition of celebrity women. It has taken over 18 months of hard work and dedication but on 6th April we staged the opening party, and the subsequent press activity has surpassed all our expectations. There were articles in most of the daily papers, magazines such as *Hello!*,

Woman's Weekly, *Eve, Woman,* as well as radio interviews. I had the pleasure to be interviewed on *GMTV...* We estimate that at least 30 million people heard about ovarian cancer as a consequence... Most importantly we are indebted to Andy and his family. It takes something special to turn personal grief into something positive and Andy and his family have benefitted many by their bravery."

Most of the women whose photographs were displayed at the exhibition had no personal link with ovarian cancer. But each recognised the importance of the cause and the need to raise awareness, as did Andy Scaysbrook. Mission accomplished? Well, nearly.

Fast forward ten years and Andy, once again, was attending an Ovacome members' day. Also at the event were Amanda Hayhurst and Juliet Morrison of Hayhurst Media who had been working with the charity as public relations and press advisors for the past year or so. The three got chatting about Ovacome's upcoming PR initiatives, Andy mentioned the exhibition of ten years previously and the seed of an idea to hold a second was planted.

That seed took a little while to propagate. At first Andy was not sure that a second exhibition would work but after more discussion, which included Louise Bayne, the then director of Ovacome, he agreed that it could work provided the theme was different to the first. To achieve that, Andy decided that this time the photographs should feature only celebrities who had been impacted personally by ovarian cancer of a family member or friend, and to include men. Also, the defining theme of the exhibition would be for each celebrity to be photographed holding a framed portrait of their loved one impacted by the disease. Latching on to that idea, Juliet suggested the exhibition should be titled 'Holding onto Hope'. This was all agreed and the 'Holding onto Hope' exhibition got underway.

The work of identifying, contacting and recruiting possible candidates for the second exhibition began in earnest. This was a delicate task as not every celebrity wanted their link to ovarian cancer publicised. Juliet spent many hours researching and speaking with individuals who, potentially, could be involved. One lucky break came early on when Hannah, the daughter of the then chairperson of Ovacome, Noëline Young, and an ovarian cancer survivor herself, persuaded the *Top Gear* presenter, James May, for whom she worked, to be part of the exhibition.

Over the next few months, 12 celebrities agreed to be part of the exhibition. This time the list included Jenny Agutter, Detmar Blow, Terri Dwyer, Nigel Havers, Chris Horridge, David Lammy MP, James May, Sam Siddall, Gwyneth Strong, Tara Palmer-Tomkinson, Carol Vorderman and Dr Sarah Wollaston MP. With the celebrities in place, Andy began preparation for the photographic sessions and Juliet worked on the publicity campaign. Through a contact of Juliet's, the team very quickly struck double gold. *The Daily Mirror* agreed to come on board and to feature the photographs in their *Celebs on Sunday* supplement to *The Sunday Mirror* newspaper, provided they were given exclusive rights to them before any other media organisation. In return, they would provide use of their Holborn Studios, known as the "Abbey Road" of photographic venues as many iconic photographs had been taken there, free of charge. This arrangement was quickly agreed by Ovacome and Andy, who could not believe his luck. Over the next few weeks, most of the photographs were taken in studio 17 of that venue although a few, by necessity, were taken in other locations. Once again, all the celebrities were gracious and generous with their time and Andy enjoyed all the sessions. But, perhaps inevitably, one stands out in his memory above all others; the session with the TV personality and socialite, Tara Palmer-Tomkinson, often known simply as TP-T.

By the time of the exhibition, TP-T's days as an "It girl" were largely over. In the mid- to late 1990s she had contributed a column to the *Sunday Times*, based on her adventures over the previous week as a socialite and well known celebrity partygoer. She contributed similar columns to several other newspapers and magazines over the years and once appeared on the cover of *Tatler* magazine under the title "It Girls". In later years she appeared on popular TV programmes including *I'm a Celebrity, Get Me Out of Here, Would I Lie to You* and *Top Gear*. Probably less known is that she co-authored several books and wrote and performed several pop songs. Also, she was a gifted pianist, appearing at the Queen Elizabeth Hall (with the National Symphony Orchestra) and at the Royal Albert Hall.

Tara had been great friends with Isabella Blow, the famous fashion icon who discovered Alexander McQueen and Sophie Dahl amongst others. Isabella, who had died in 2007, had been an ovarian cancer sufferer, her death being a huge blow to Tara as well as Isabella's husband, Detmar, who had also agreed to be photographed for the exhibition. Tara had many abiding memories of Isabella, including having Sunday lunches at her home, arriving in jeans and leaving in haute couture!

On the day of her "shoot", TP-T arrived at the studio with her own make-up artist and a huge quantity of burgers from a local McDonalds. She did not want anyone to be hungry! Noticing the piano in the studio, Tara quickly went over to it and began to play at which point Andy suggested that maybe they should listen to some music during the shoot. To his surprise, Tara pulled out of her handbag a CD of her own songs, titled *Flawed*, which had just been recorded and told Andy to play her favourite track: 'Lapin de Neige' (Snow Rabbit). Tara had brought along several portraits of Isabella and a beautiful hat made by Phillip Treacy, another great friend of Tara's and a big supporter of Ovacome which she quickly donned. The image was set up with Tara appearing to bite the corner of the portrait's frame and one of the most iconic photographs of the exhibition, perhaps of British portrait photography, was taken.

The next challenge was to find a venue to host the exhibition. After several failed attempts to find one, the Menier Gallery in Southwark, London (nicknamed "the chocolate factory" because it used to be one), offered its basement space which was perfect. The exhibition launch date was set for the 2nd March 2012, some ten months after Andy, Juliet and Amanda met at

Ovacome's May 2011 members' day. Andy's son, Louis, was due to attend but was ill and could not make the trip but his father did make the journey from Coventry to be there. Father and son met, had lunch and then visited the gallery to view the exhibition. Up until that point, Andy had been in "professional" mode but walking around the gallery, the emotion hit both he and his father; some tears were shed.

TP-T vamps it for the camera.
– Holding onto Hope exhibition, March 2012.
Courtesy of Andy Scaybrook.

Nigel Havers holding a photograph of his wife.
– Holding onto Hope exhibition 2012.
Courtesy of Andy Scaysbrook.

Louis Russell - Scaysbrook holding a photograph
of the grandmother he never met.
– Holding onto Hope exhibition, March 2012.
Courtesy of Andy Scaysbrook

Andy Scaysbrook and Tara Palmer-Tomkinson.
– Holding onto Hope exhibition, March 2012.

Jenny Agutter, Ovacome's Patron, holding a photograph
of Louise Bayne, then CEO of Ovacome with her daughter.
– Holding onto Hope exhibition, March 2012.
Courtesy of Andy Scaysbrook

Later that evening, members and staff of the charity mingled with some of the celebrities who were there, including Jenny Agutter, the chef, Chris Horridge, and the actress, Gwyneth Strong. As well as exhibiting thirteen portraits, one of each of the 12 celebrities involved, plus Andy's son holding a portrait of his grandmother, an auction was held of memorabilia donated by celebrities. Items offered to the highest bidder included a tie donated by Nigel Havers, a bottle of champagne signed by then Prime Minister, David Cameron, and a 30cm high red hat donated by Philip Treacy. The man with the hammer was no less than Mark Stacey, antiques expert and *Bargain Hunt* presenter. The auction was in full flow when, as if cued by a stage manager, TP-T swept into the room wearing a glittering, figure hugging, gold dress. By amazing coincidence, Mark had just began to auction a copy of Tara's CD, *Flawed*. He hardly missed a beat as he announced, "as if straight from Hollywood, here she is." Tara quickly took up the microphone and, together with Mark, helped to raise over £1200 for Ovacome.

Just prior to the exhibition, on 26th February, *The Sunday Mirror* published their promised feature in the *Celebs on Sunday* supplement, which, at that time, had 1.3 million readers. The six page spread included photographs and comments from five of the celebrities involved plus information on the symptoms of ovarian cancer and how Ovacome was working to raise awareness of the disease. Mel Brodie, editor of the supplement, said of the exhibition: "Loss and hope, emotion and beauty are combined in Andy Scaysbrook's captivating portraits. He photographed some of the UK's most famous names who tell the story about a loved one they have lost, or who suffered from ovarian cancer. A collection well worth seeing and a charity well worth supporting".

In the days and weeks following the event, it was featured in many other newspapers and magazines whilst Jenny Agutter appeared on national TV talking about the exhibition and the charity. Overall, the publicity achieved was another major boost to Ovacome's profile and reputation. The following year, the exhibition was displayed in the public library in Brighton, achieving still more publicity and goodwill. Juliet Morrison interviewed each of the twelve celebrities taking part and a book, titled *Holding onto Hope* was produced which contained the twelve portraits chosen for the exhibition plus Juliet's commentary based on her interviews. The book was put on sale, raising more funds for Ovacome.

Fittingly, the final words about the exhibition come from Andy Scaysbrook: "I know how devastating ovarian cancer can be to families from first-hand experience, with the impact it has had on my dad, my brother and my son, Louis, who was born shortly after Mum passed away. I talk to Louis about Mum every day and so he feels as if he knows her but it's such a shame he never got to meet my best friend".

Over a decade or so, Andy Scaysbrook's photographic talent and enthusiasm had placed ovarian cancer and Ovacome in front of literally millions of people across the UK and abroad. It was a massive contribution and result for which the charity is and always will be, grateful.

Chapter 4A

DIAGNOSIS AND TREATMENT –
A BRIEF HISTORY.
2000-2010

Diagnosis:

Little significant progress in diagnosing ovarian cancer was made during the first ten years of the new century, except for advances in CT and MRI scanning that improved the understanding of the nature, grading and staging of an individual's disease during and after diagnosis.

Treatment:

However, the advances in treatment were more dynamic and progressive, with the introduction of new types of drugs (especially in the second half of the decade) and positive evidence of the efficacy of specific chemotherapy and surgical processes heralding a more promising era for sufferers.

By the start of the new century, the introduction of platinum-based chemotherapy (in the 1970s) had led to treatments that were differentiated between those patients that responded to this therapy (platinum-sensitive patients) and those who did not (platinum-resistant patients). Treatments had also become more individualised between those who were diagnosed for the first time and others whose cancer had recurred after initial treatment.

One potentially promising treatment being researched and trialled in the late 1990s and early 2000s was high-dose chemotherapy (HDCT) with peripheral stem cell transplant. This clinical technique, that had been used for treating blood cancers and some breast cancers for several years, aimed to overcome drug resistance by increasing the dosages of the chemotherapy drugs infused. Whilst potentially effective in killing cancer cells that had been resistant to more normal levels of chemotherapy, the level of drugs involved also killed many other, non-cancerous, cells. Put simply, this challenge was overcome by the extraction of stem cells (basic building blocks of life that can transform themselves into other forms of cells that the body needs) from the patient's blood, prior to HDCT commencing and then reinfusing them a few days after treatment. These stem cells then went on to develop into all the other healthy cells the body needs. Trials of this approach were run in the USA, UK and other European countries but ultimately proved to be inconclusive and HDCT/stem cell transplant did not enter the oncologists' treatment armoury in any significant way.

Also, in the late 1990s/ early 2000s a drug, named docetaxel, emerged as an alternative to paclitaxel, then the standard first line treatment drug, usually combined with either carboplatin or cisplatin. Docetaxel was a semi-synthetic drug derived from European yew (similar to paclitaxel) which demonstrated similar efficacy but lower levels of neurotoxicity, for example tingling or numbness of the hands in some patients. Several trials of docetaxel were held internationally, and the drug continues to be an option two decades later, particularly for those who suffer more from neurotoxic side effects.

Possibly one of the most important advances in understanding (and, therefore, treating) cancer including ovarian, in the first few years of the new century, was the sequencing of the genome of tumours. A major study of genome sequencing commenced in 1997 with the launch of the Cancer Genome Atlas Project (CGAP) by the National Cancer Institute of America. By 2003 the CGAP project was able to publish the largest publicly available collection of cancer "expressed sequence tags", essentially giving oncologists and scientists an understanding of the genetic structure of individual tumour types. In parallel, in 2000, the Sanger Institute, part of the Wellcome Trust in the UK, launched its "Cancer Genome Project" with the goal of advancing the understanding of cancer genomes and the mutations that occur as cancer cells develop. All this work provided a foundation for the more targeted and personalised treatments that were to be developed and introduced in the years ahead.

Two approaches to treatment became the subject of considerable debate in the middle of the decade. The first concerned the question of whether patients with the disease should have surgery, followed by chemotherapy (the standard approach in most cases), or to reverse, at least partially, that order. In December 2004, Sean Kehoe, then Professor of Gynaecological Cancer at Oxford University (and later to become the chair of Ovacome's medical advisory body), wrote an article for Ovacome's newsletter describing a clinical trial being undertaken at 87 hospitals across the UK and New Zealand, called "CHemotherapy OR Upfront Surgery" (CHORUS). Sean explained that the trial would randomly assign patients with advanced ovarian cancer (stage 3 or 4) to one of two treatment groups. Patients in the first group would undergo the normal process of surgery followed by chemotherapy; in the second, chemotherapy would be the first line of treatment (known as adjuvant chemotherapy), followed by surgery and then more chemotherapy, an approach already used by some doctors. Over a six-year period, 552 patients were assigned to the trial and the results were closely monitored for differences in surgical outcome, side effects and overall survival. The trial demonstrated there to be no significant variation in outcomes overall, but that adjuvant chemotherapy could reduce the size of larger tumours, making surgery a less extensive procedure for both patient and surgeon. Subsequently the results of the CHORUS study were combined with a European trial (EORTC 55971) and taken together they confirmed a better survival outcome for the adjuvant chemotherapy technique in those with stage 4 disease.

The overall conclusion was for doctors to review each individual case, particularly the stage of the disease, and discuss treatment options with the patient. Similar results and conclusions were found in other trials completed in several countries, including the USA and Canada.

The second concerned whether infusing chemotherapy drugs directly into the abdomen (intraperitoneal) delivered improved overall outcomes for advanced ovarian cancer sufferers than the more standard approach of infusing through a vein in the arm (intravenous). In 2006, the National Cancer Institute in the USA encouraged the use of combined IP and IV chemotherapy, following surgery, for patients with advanced disease. This recommendation was based on the results of a large trial completed by a research network known as the Gynaecologic Oncology Group (GOG), led by Doctor Deborah Armstrong. However, quite soon, both the NCI recommendation and the underlying evidence presented by GOG, became the subject of medical debate, with several eminent oncologists, including Professor Martin Gore of the Royal Marsden hospital, questioning several aspects of the trial.

The GOG trial gained some support from a further study known as PETROC/OV21 which was multi-country and included the involvement of Cancer Research UK. This trial, held between 2009 and 2016, involved 275 patients who had previously received platinum-based chemotherapy, followed by surgery. The trial concluded that there was some evidence to suggest that a combination of intraperitoneal and intravenous infusion led to improved overall outcomes. Unfortunately, the numbers involved in the trial were not large enough to lead to a firm conclusion regarding an improvement in overall survival rates.

The discussion as to which was more effective: IP infusion; a combination of IP and IV; or IV alone, continued over the next decade without full resolution. Nonetheless, intraperitoneal chemotherapy continued to be used by doctors in the USA and, gradually, the technique was improved and is an option for some patients in the UK with relevant clinical indications. Perhaps a little confusingly for patients, some oncologists became, and still are, quite strong supporters of the technique and others are much less enthusiastic. Evidence that medicine is not an exact science.

And then, right at the end of the decade, the most significant development in drug therapy of the entire ten-year period occurred with the publication of the results of a stage 3 trial in the USA (GOG218) of a drug named bevacizumab, developed and marketed under the name "Avastin" by Genentech, a subsidiary of the giant Swiss pharmaceutical company, Roche. Avastin was a new type of drug, a "monoclonal antibody" that targeted a cancer cell protein called "vascular endothelial growth factor" (VEGF). VEGF is essential to the ability of cancer cells to grow new blood vessels and Avastin blocked, or at least reduced, that ability so that cancer cells died or grew less rapidly. Already in use for several types of cancer, the trial suggested a positive impact in the treatment of advanced ovarian cancer when administered together with standard chemotherapy drugs, but the results were not conclusive.

Nonetheless, in 2012, the European Medicines Agency (EMA) approved the use of Avastin for first line treatment in patients with the disease. As a result of that approval, Avastin became available in England through the (recently introduced) Cancer Drugs Fund and doctors in other parts of the UK were able to apply for funding for its use. However, the National Institute for Clinical Excellence (NICE) had yet to approve the drug for general use across the NHS. Avastin appeared to be a breakthrough, a "wonder drug" even, but, as so often in medicine, further research qualified that assessment.

Another phase 3 trial of Avastin, this time involving 263 hospitals across many countries (but not the USA), was carried out between 2006 and 2009. This trial, known as ICON 7, reported interim results in 2011, followed by final results in 2013. Whilst the interim analysis suggested similar results to the GOG218 trial, the final results reported no significant improvement in overall survival rates. The exception to that conclusion was for those with high-risk disease who did achieve better overall survival periods. In 2013, based on the evidence available at that time, NICE issued guidance that Avastin, in combination with carboplatin and paclitaxel, should not be recommended for first line treatment of ovarian cancer. Further trials combining Avastin with several types of chemotherapy drug have been completed or are in progress in more recent years, including the OCEAN and AURELIA trials.

Whilst the ultimate efficacy of Avastin, in combination with standard chemotherapy drugs, remains the subject of medical debate it did, at least, provide an important insight into drugs which had a targeted effect on cancerous cells alone (or mostly) as opposed to standard chemotherapy treatments which impacted a much broader range of cells in the body, malignant or not. Much more development of these types of drugs was to come in the second decade of the 21st century.

Chapter 5

CONSENSUS LEADS TO BEAT

Consensus

Why is ovarian cancer so difficult to diagnosis at an early stage? Many cancers are insidious; they hide their effect, progress quite slowly, show few, if any, observable symptoms until relatively advanced, pretend to be something else, something less concerning. Few more so than ovarian cancer.

This simple truth was complicated further by the fact that, even as late as 2005, medical professionals, particularly GPs, did not have a common set of agreed symptoms that would point directly towards the real possibility of an ovarian cancer diagnosis. Routine screening for the disease was not (and, in 2021, is not) available.

This issue was taken head on by Ovacome, together with another charity, the Eve Appeal, who decided to hold a meeting of experts and relevant charities to determine if a "Consensus Statement" on symptoms and early detection could be achieved. A similar document existed in the USA, agreed between the American Cancer Society, the Gynaecological Cancer Foundation and the Society of Gynaecological Oncologists in 2007, which set out a list of symptoms frequently seen in ovarian cancer.

The meeting was held on the 8th April 2008 at the QE II conference centre, close to the Houses of Parliament, as part of the "Institute for Women's Health" annual conference that year. It was chaired by Professor Mike Richards, then the national clinical director for cancer. The first part of the meeting was an open forum, attended by members of the charities involved: Ovacome, The Eve Appeal, Ovarian Cancer Action and Well Being of Women. Four eminent doctors each gave a presentation on a specific aspect of the disease and its symptoms, followed by senior representatives of the charities present and other health professionals, who added their perspectives. Louise Bayne, then director of Ovacome, spoke from the patients' viewpoint, drawing generally on the ten years' experience of the charity in supporting individuals with the disease, and presenting compelling evidence from a survey of 400 members, completed in 2006. This demonstrated, for example, the shocking fact that it took on average, three to four GP appointments before a patient was referred to a consultant. Following the open forum, and after a short break, the medical professionals convened in a closed session to draft the Consensus Statement.

By autumn, the statement had been drafted, reviewed, amended and issued in final format. As well as setting out guidelines to help both women and medical practitioners identify symptoms, the statement highlighted gaps in research into the disease and suggested actions to fill those gaps. Whilst an important document in its own right, the Consensus Statement spawned several other initiatives, furthering the understanding of the disease. For example, it was input to a then current Department of Health initiative to develop ovarian cancer key messages; *The Times* newspaper ran an online debate on health issues and Louise Bayne was invited to be its first author; a research interest group was established to help decide priorities. And two years later the statement was part of the foundations of a new awareness campaign launched by Ovacome, called "BEAT".

BEAT

BEAT was simple in concept, but very powerful in action. It was based on the well understood fact that most of us find it much easier to remember an idea, or a list of symptoms, if a memorable acronym is created to prompt the memory. Such was BEAT in describing the symptoms of ovarian cancer:

- Bloating that is persistent and does not come and go
- Eating less and feeling fuller afterwards
- Abdominal pain that persists
- Toilet; needing to go more frequently and/or changes in bowel habit, (initially T stood for "tell your doctor" but was changed to toilet when urinary/bowel habit became a more recognised symptom of ovarian cancer)

Ovacome's BEAT symptom awareness message was conceived and developed by the charity's PR consultants at the time, building on the work that had led to the Consensus Statement. It was set to become one of the biggest awareness campaigns ever run by Ovacome.

The campaign was launched at a press conference, held for women's magazine health editors in November 2009, hosted by Jenny Agutter, Ovacome's patron, together with Professor Mike Richards, national cancer director, and Professor Sean Kehoe of Oxford University. Hot on the heels of that event, Ovacome placed symptom awareness stories in many leading magazine titles, including *Good Housekeeping*, *Red*, and *Cosmopolitan*.

But the programme took on massive impetus in March 2010 (chosen to coincide with ovarian cancer awareness month) from harnessing the power of its own membership. Every member was asked to enlist the help of their local GP practice by encouraging them to become a "BEAT-friendly surgery" and to display a BEAT poster in their patient waiting room. In tandem, the charity arranged to work with the Royal College of General Practitioners in a three-year international project to input the latest research findings into practice to promote earlier diagnosis. As a further boost to the campaign, an interactive web-based tool was introduced that provided an improved understanding of the risks of developing the disease, plus a "track and record symptoms" capability. This could be taken to a GP appointment to help with discussion and diagnosis. The tool was improved further the following year when a company called "Health Unlocked", founded by clinicians to assist doctors and their patients, developed its capability and integrated a genetic risk factor module. The resulting tool was the most advanced and comprehensive available and helped women with both their own observations and interactions with their GP.

A short film, introduced by Jenny Agutter and featuring two of Ovacome's members, was made and placed on YouTube as well as Ovacome's website; small cards carrying the BEAT message were produced and distributed to members to be handed out at events, or at any other opportunity; overseas charities in Australia, Canada and the USA were approached and invited to take up the BEAT campaign.

Over the next few months, BEAT, and Ovacome more generally, received unprecedented levels of press coverage across the spectrum of women's magazines and daily national newspapers. Many of the charity's members spoke to their local press and media on the back of the initiative, leading to even more of the public becoming aware of the BEAT message. But perhaps the most poignant article of all appeared in *Good Housekeeping*'s June 2010 issue, featuring Michèle Dickinson, the daughter of Sarah, the charity's founder. Only four years old when her mother died in 1997, Michèle, by now a young adult, spoke of her mother's determination to set up a support group for all those affected by ovarian cancer. She went on to say, "Mum was able to see the charity flourish before she died. Going through life without Mum has not been easy, and special occasions are particularly difficult. My greatest comfort has been a journal Mum made for me before she passed away. Mum wrote down her thoughts and feelings so that I could get to know her. She told me about the people she admired and left presents with my father to give me on my special birthdays. For my sixteenth birthday, she left me an engraved locket that had a picture of us together. The keepsakes she left me and the work she did for ovarian cancer mean that a part of her still lives on".

A few months later, Louise Bayne attended a conference of the International Gynaecological Cancer Society in Prague. The conference attracted over 2500 attendees, many of whom visited the Ovacome stand which was dedicated largely to the BEAT campaign. By this time, BEAT had been adopted by similar charities in Australia and New Zealand and the USA was keen to come on board. Canada was already promoting the initiative to its English speaking population. Several other countries across Europe, Asia and the Middle East were showing interest. An international coalition under the headline title "BEAT Worldwide" was taking shape.

Ovacome's heroines and heroes – Louise Bayne

Louise Bayne, a midwife, first knew of Ovacome through reading Sarah Dickinson's (the charity's founder) article in Good Housekeeping *magazine, published in early 1996. It coincided with a period in her own life that her husband, Duncan, described as the best and worst six weeks of their lives. Their first child, a son, was two weeks old, Duncan had just passed a surgeon's exam and an ultrasound scan had identified that a cyst, monitored through Louise's pregnancy, might be more worrying. The inevitable surgical procedure was undertaken and the result suggested borderline ovarian cancer. Six months, and a house move, later, abdominal pain forced Louise back to hospital for scans and investigations and she started a close monitoring regime that was to last another two years. During this time, Louise noticed another article about Ovacome and decided to attend the next AGM. Shortly after, she signed up to be part of the raising awareness task force, a Fone Friend, and joined the charity's committee in 1998.*

Over the next year, Louise's symptoms worsened and it became obvious that she would need a hysterectomy and removal of her ovaries. Surgery was scheduled but, miracles of miracles, Louise fell pregnant just before the planned date. A further near miracle occurred when a scan showed no evidence of a tumour, and the pregnancy was able to go full term with the birth of a daughter. The planned surgery was completed a few months later and, to Duncan and Louise's great relief, the tumour was found to be benign. At that time Louise wrote: "Through Ovacome I have met so many wonderful, brave, determined women (and men), who continue to inspire. If ovarian cancer is my dark cloud, then Ovacome is a very bright silver lining".

In the autumn of 1999, Madeleine Gold, then chair of Ovacome, stood down as she was moving abroad, and Louise stepped into her shoes. Three years later, Ovacome's growth had been so rapid that a decision was taken to appoint a director to run the day-to-day operations of the charity, whilst maintaining the chairperson role as oversight. Louise became the first director (the title was changed to chief executive officer in 2006) and held that role for the next 15 years. Finally, in late 2017, Louise stepped down from her long and dedicated involvement with Ovacome as her husband had accepted a position in New Zealand and the family emigrated.

Over a near 20-year period Louise, together with the trustee board members across that timeframe, had shaped and guided Ovacome from a fledgling start-up to a respected and highly regarded charity, a leader in the field of ovarian cancer support. Her professional status as a

97

midwife gave her access to the medical community and she made this a priority. Her goal was to ensure that Ovacome was an asset to the doctors, nurses and related medical professionals working with ovarian cancer, in addition to all those with the disease, their families and friends. As such, she attended numerous conferences, meetings and seminars, helping to bridge the technical language barrier between medical staff and patients.

During her tenure, Louise introduced and oversaw numerous initiatives and programmes, many of which are detailed elsewhere in this book. Key amongst them were: introduction of the telephone counselling service; opening the first dedicated office of the charity; multiple improvements and reiterations of factsheets and other information material, written by leading clinicians; two major photographic exhibitions; Survivors Teaching Students (STS) programme; online symptom tracker and, later, clinical trial finder; the Consensus Statement, leading to the BEAT campaign.

A major contribution to the charity's success.

The second wave of the BEAT campaign, "Teal Tips", was introduced in March 2011 with an innovative promotion of teal coloured (teal being the colour associated with ovarian cancer) nail polish. The polish had been developed by leading brand OPI and named "Ski Teal We Drop". Fronted by Jenny Agutter, pictured wearing the varnish, each bottle sold came with a leaflet explaining BEAT. Kindly, OPI donated £1 to the charity for every bottle sold. Such was the success of the initiative that it was repeated every March for the next seven years, with a new varnish featured at each anniversary (the manufacturer changed from OPI to Barry M in 2013) and a range of celebrities adding their endorsement and support. For Ovacome the Teal Tips campaign generated many thousands of pounds of much needed funds and helped to raise the awareness of ovarian cancer.

Since 2010, the BEAT message has been promoted in many ways; from organised centralised campaigns, through locally arranged events, to one individual speaking to another. Unquestionably it has led to a greater awareness of the symptoms of the disease amongst the public as a whole and resulted in countless numbers of women seeking medical advice earlier than they would otherwise have done, saving or prolonging lives and, often, preventing needless worry. More than a decade later, BEAT continues to be a simple, memorable and powerful communicator:

- Bloating that is persistent and does not come and go
- Eating less and feeling fuller afterwards
- Abdominal pain that persists
- Toilet; needing to go more frequently and/or changes in bowel habit

Please make a mental note.

Chapter 6

MEMORIES FOR MEDICS

Charing Cross Hospital and Medical School in London has a long and illustrious history. Its origins lie in the founding of the "West London Infirmary and Dispensary" at 16 Suffolk Street, London in 1818, driven by the vision of Dr Benjamin Golding to establish a healing place for the poor. The hospital flourished and three years later the facilities were relocated to Villiers Street, London, close to Charing Cross station. One year later a medical school was opened alongside the hospital.

Fittingly, in 1827, the name was changed to the "Charing Cross Hospital" and a site was identified near The Strand, less than a mile from the station, for a brand new building to house both patients and medical students. The new hospital was opened in 1834, the first ward named after then princess, but later queen, Victoria. The hospital and medical school continued to expand and following the Second World War, a proposal was made to relocate away from central London. It would take a further decade before a decision was finalised and a location – that of the existing Fulham Hospital on Fulham Palace Road, West London, confirmed. The decision was controversial with local people, and it took years of meetings and discussions before building could commence. Finally, the new hospital, in the shape of a cross and 17 storeys high, was opened formally by Queen Elizabeth II on May 22nd 1973. It had cost a then huge £15 million to build and equip and was one of the most modern in the world.

It was here, in May 2014, that an exciting and important new chapter opened in the life of Ovacome with the inaugural session of a programme of members of the charity meeting directly with medical students to talk about their experiences of ovarian cancer. This programme was titled "Survivors Teaching Students" or simply "STS".

The STS programme had its origins in the USA and was owned and trademarked by the Ovarian Cancer National Alliance of America. It had been running for several years when Louise Bayne, recently appointed as Ovacome's first director, attended an international conference of ovarian cancer charity leaders held in New York in the summer of 2001. The STS programme was on the agenda and Louise had a good opportunity to talk to other attendees and gain an understanding of how it worked. After her return to the UK, Louise frequently thought about the programme and how it could benefit medical students at home. But Ovacome's resources were limited and there were many other initiatives to push ahead during the so-called "noughties". Consequently, STS remained on Ovacome's back burner until the passing of a young doctor from the disease quickly brought it forward onto the front burner.

Ovacome's Heroines and Heroes – Dr Lisa-Jayne Clark's (and her family's) story

Lisa-Jayne Clark had three great passions in life: family (husband, daughter, parents and sisters), medicine... And pop festivals! Born in Poughkeepsie, New York State (Roger, her father, was on an assignment there) in 1972, her childhood moved between the USA, UK and Canada. Back in the UK, from her mid-teens she studied for A levels at Barton Peveril College in Eastleigh, Hampshire and then studied medicine at the Charing Cross and Westminster Medical School. Her early years as a doctor took her to hospitals across the UK where she demonstrated her love of medicine, and compassion for her fellow woman and man; whilst still a student Lisa had been thrilled to win an international award from the BALINT society, an organisation dedicated to helping doctors better understand and relate to their patients emotional, as well as clinical, needs. Lisa's mother, Lyn, recalls travelling to Sandbanks, near Poole, Dorset, where her daughter was working in a local hospital, to celebrate her birthday. Sitting outside a coffee shop, waiting for the chain ferry that crosses the mouth of Poole harbour and links Sandbanks with Swanage and Bournemouth, Lisa heard that a bus had overturned on the other side of the water. Immediately she left her mother and rushed to the scene to help the injured, returning some four hours later, exhausted.

As part of her medical training Lisa also travelled to the other side of the world, visiting and working in New Zealand and the Tongan island of Vava'u. It was on this island that Lisa delivered her first baby, a girl; a very moving experience for her. She wrote regularly in her diary and would often mention that her mother and father would love a particular sight or location. During one trip to Australia Lisa sent her father a birthday postcard with a picture of an emperor penguin. She did not know it at the time, but that postcard was destined to trigger a chain of events in later years.

Through her work Lisa encountered an organisation called Festival Medical Services that provided doctors and other health care staff at music festivals around the UK. Quite quickly Lisa became their clinical lead, attending many of the festivals. Through the thickest mud and the most brilliant sunshine, she and her colleagues tended to the sick, the injured, or the merely worse for wear amongst the festivalgoers.

It was during one of those festivals, Glastonbury, June 2011, that Lisa first felt a little unwell. The weather in the days leading up to the event had seen a lot of heavy rain and the car parks and main site were very muddy. More rain fell during the first two days of the festival, only clearing to blue skies and sunshine on the final day (Sunday). "Glasto" was very popular that year (attaining its highest TV audience to that date) as the headline acts on the main Pyramid Stage were U2, Coldplay and Beyonce on the Friday, Saturday and Sunday evenings respectively.

By now a consultant in emergency medicine, Lisa was at Glasto with her husband, Simon, 10-month-old baby daughter, Lucy, and her parents. As usual, the festival was hard work for the medical team and Lisa attributed her chest pains, tiredness and feeling of being bloated as nothing more than the result of being a new mother, trudging up and down the site hills in the mud and working too hard. But on the Saturday evening, Lisa felt too ill to watch her favourite band, Coldplay, perform. Clearly something was wrong.

In the days following her return home, the symptoms grew steadily worse and Lisa felt sick much of the time. One night she half-laughingly suggested to Simon (a radiologist) that she had ascites (fluid in the stomach), never a good thing. The following day she decided to get a private ultrasound scan after work which confirmed the ascites and a large swelling on her ovary. Two days later and following a visit to her GP, Lucy met a gynaecological consultant who confirmed that exploratory surgery was required and ordered blood tests and an MRI scan. It was then that Lisa realised that despite being a highly qualified and experienced doctor, she had not recognised the classic symptoms of ovarian cancer. The MRI scan happened quickly and was followed by a meeting with a different consultant and a CT scan. The next day Lisa was admitted to hospital and underwent six hours of surgery, removing both ovaries, uterus and surrounding tissue. The following week, in hospital, was a very difficult time for Lisa. As a doctor, she understood the extent and seriousness of her disease and found it difficult to eat and sleep, feeling weak and losing confidence. Not surprisingly, when the time came to leave hospital, she was exhausted and anxious. However, she knew these were normal conditions and vowed to herself to get better and stronger quickly.

First line chemotherapy started about six weeks later in August 2011. As was normal practice the first line drugs were a combination of carboplatin and paclitaxel; Lisa underwent six cycles ending in November, losing her hair along the way. The results were good with her CA125 level falling from around 320 to 11, well within the normal range. A visit to her oncologist just prior to Christmas was also positive, the consultant giving an all-clear opinion. Hope was restored, but not for long.

Immediately following Christmas, Lisa, Simon and Lucy took a short holiday at a cottage they had rented in Devon. It was a lovely few days for the family with much walking and even swimming. Sadly, during the time in Devon, Lisa discovered a lump in her neck. Blood tests and scans the following week confirmed that the cancer was back, just six weeks after treatment had ended. Devastating news.

Within a few weeks, Lisa had been enrolled on the OSI-906 trial being administered at the Royal Marsden hospital in London under Professor Martin Gore, one of the most respected oncologists in the world and a big supporter of Ovacome. OSI-906 was trialling the impact on recurred ovarian cancer of a combination of the drugs carboplatin and linsitinib, an experimental medication at that time. Unfortunately, the trial had no positive effect for Lisa (and was later discontinued due to low efficacy) and her cancer spread to her liver and bowel. A further experimental drug, myocet, was tried in combination with carboplatin but, again, no positive response was seen.

Lisa was fortunate in that she had a very loving family to turn to during her illness. Not only her husband, mother and father, but her two sisters, Amanda and Jenni, who both provided constant comfort and love. As Amanda lived relatively close by, she had been able to visit her sister frequently, providing both physical and emotional support. Jenni lived on the west coast of America but spoke to Lisa as often as possible and flew to the UK to be with her on several occasions.

Happily, some relief from her illness was to arrive through the spring and summer. In May, Lisa turned 40 years old. To celebrate she and Simon rented an eight-bedroom cottage, complete with swimming pool and hot tub, in Devon and invited family and friends – many from her student days – to a fancy dress birthday party. Dinner was served and much wine was drunk and soon it turned into a medical school reunion party with hilarious stories of student days past being traded around the table. After dinner, the dancing kicked in until, finally, everyone collapsed with exhausted joy as the morning sun peeped over the horizon.

In June, Lisa and her sister, Amanda, went to see Coldplay perform in Manchester and, through the efforts of their sister, Jenni (who worked with a member of Coldplay's staff), they were able to meet the band backstage prior to the concert. The moment arrived and the band appeared. Photographs were taken, autographs given, and Lisa had a memorable chat with Chris Martin, lead singer with the band, who knew of her circumstances. Somewhat starstruck they returned to the centre of the stadium and "rock and rolled" to Coldplay's set.

Two months later, on 2nd September, Amanda married her fiancé, Barry. By now, Lisa was very ill and had recently undergone several sessions of radiotherapy to *relieve pressure and pain in her back as the cancer had spread there. But she was determined to be at her sister's wedding and for Lucy, who had turned two years old a couple of weeks earlier, to be the "belle of the ball", acting as flower girl to Amanda.*

During her final days, Lisa was moved to St Wilfred's hospice in Chichester where her father, Roger, took her some mail. The last piece of mail she ever read was a card from Chris Martin, Gwyneth Paltrow and their children - it said, "I hope you are OK, stay strong, it was wonderful to meet you".

Two days later, one month after Amanda's wedding, Tuesday 2nd October 2012, Lisa died.

In common with Ovacome's founder, Sarah Dickinson, Lisa wanted desperately to leave memories and messages for her daughter to have and read at the right time. She wrote an intimate account of her childhood, student days, early career and cancer experience, writing in the first person to her beloved Lucy; an account that, later, Lisa's parents had produced as a book. After her funeral, family and friends contributed personal items to a "memories box", full of treasures and mementoes for Lucy to enjoy in the future. Lisa's memory would endure.

During her illness, Lisa had read about Ovacome and became a member, obtaining information from the charity and connecting with others in a similar situation. She would say often that through these connections she felt "not alone". In her final weeks, Lisa requested her parents do two things after her death. The first was for them to ensure that her memory lived on, so she was not forgotten, especially by Lucy as she grew up. The second was to support Ovacome in any way possible and to donate funds raised in her memory to the charity. Fulfilling those wishes became Roger and Lyn's focus in the months and years ahead.

Two weeks after Lisa's funeral, Roger woke in the middle of the night with a question going around his mind, together with a possible answer. He and Lyn knew that Lisa loved to travel, so taking a trip in her memory felt like a good thing to do; plus, funding was possible due to a legacy that Lisa had left them. The question was: where would they most like to go if they had only one chance to make an adventurous trip? As Roger was a keen wildlife photographer and fan of David Attenborough, the answer seemed obvious: Antarctica to photograph penguins in their natural and, to humans, hostile habitat. And then a strange thing happened. On looking through one of his travel books, the card that Lisa had sent Roger for his birthday some years earlier fell out and there, staring him in the face, was an adult penguin and her chick. It seemed that Lisa was giving her blessing to the planned voyage.

The trip took several months to plan but in November 2013, Roger and Lyn travelled to the Falklands and South Georgia where Roger spent several happy, if cold, days photographing penguins. Arriving back in the UK, Roger looked more closely at Lisa's card and realised, somewhat to his horror, that he had photographed the wrong penguins. The adult penguin and chick depicted on the postcard were emperors, the largest members of the species. He had photographed king penguins, the second largest. There was only one thing to do; return to Antarctica and photograph the right birds!

After much planning, Roger made the return trip in late 2016, this time without his wife, Lyn, staying three days at Gould Bay, on the Weddell Sea. Over that time, in temperatures that varied between a "balmy" minus 6 degrees centigrade, and a "brutal" minus 30 degrees, he managed to capture many exhilarating shots of the emperors, both adult and young, individually and in large groups. At the point that he captured his first photographs, Roger called Lyn by satellite phone to share the moment and then etched Lisa's name in the snow. Finally, the objective had been achieved.

Two years later, Roger and Lyn undertook one further memorable but long and arduous journey in memory of their daughter. This time they decided to follow in Lisa's footsteps and visit the Northlands of New Zealand and the Tongan island of Vava'u where she had delivered her first baby, who was to be named Lisa in her honour. Roger had learned also of a rare member of the penguin family, the royal penguin, which existed only on Macquarie Island, near Tasmania, so a trip was developed to join an expedition to Macquarie, add photographs of the royal to the emperor and king penguins already captured on film, trace Lisa's footsteps in New Zealand and, if possible, find the baby named after their daughter, who she had delivered and would now be 21 years old.

Roger and Lyn set out on December 15th 2018, and returned one month later, having travelled over 30,000 miles. The highlight of the trip was undoubtedly the visit to Vava'u, where, with the help of local people, they visited the hospital that Lisa had worked in, and managed to locate and meet the "baby", now young adult, Lisa had delivered 21 years previously, plus her extended family – a deeply emotional moment.

Roger and Lyn met the family a couple of more times before making their final visit of the journey, to the hotel that Lisa had stayed at: the Paradise Hotel. By then largely derelict, they were able to locate and stand in the room and on the balcony that Lisa had written about in such joyous terms in 1997. As they slowly shut the door to room number 115, they experienced a deep and stirring sense of personal closure. They had followed in their daughter's footsteps, seen what she wanted them to see and touched on her foreign experiences.

Completing their travels had been a fundamental part of Roger and Lyn honouring their daughter's memory. But of equal importance was honouring her wish to aid Ovacome in any way possible. During and shortly after Lisa's funeral, donations had been made by mourners, friends and colleagues in her memory. In total £7700 was raised, including a cheque for £2500 from Festival Medical Services in recognition of the contribution she had made to their cause.

In keeping with Lisa's wishes, this money was to be given to Ovacome but Roger and Lyn were keen that it should be used for a specific purpose, not as general funds. They discussed this with Louise Bayne who proposed that the money should be directed at setting up the STS programme in the UK. Roger and Lyn were enthusiastic about this proposal and in July 2013 Ruth Grigg, at that time the volunteer and information manager of the charity, travelled to Washington DC to be trained in STS.

On her return to the UK, Ruth began the process of planning the implementation of STS into UK hospitals and medical schools. Members of the charity were contacted to establish if they would be willing to talk to medical students about their symptoms, diagnosis and treatment. Although a potentially difficult and emotional experience there was no lack of volunteers as very many members could envision the benefits of such a programme. A short film was produced to be used at the opening of each session, featuring Jenny Agutter, Ovacome's patron, and Roger and Lyn talking about Lisa's life and the STS project. Coldplay were approached for permission to use their music as soundtrack to the film which they readily gave. Lisa's alma mater, the Charing Cross and Westminster Medical School, was approached and asked if they would be the location of the first STS event which, again, was quickly agreed.

Lisa at Glastonbury, June 2011.

Roger Clark photographing Emperor penguins in Antarctica, 2016.
Courtesy of Sue Bart

Richard Stock finishing the London Marathon, 2014, raising
£4,000 for the Survivors Teaching Students programme.

By May 2014 the scene was set for that first event and three Ovacome members were ready to present to, and talk with, medical students in a live setting. Jenny Agutter addressed the students, explaining why and how she became involved with Ovacome and the film was played. The three presenters spoke movingly about their experiences of diagnosis, treatment and living with ovarian cancer, driving home crucial information that would, hopefully, help to improve outcomes for others in the future. Unfortunately, not one of the presenters had received an early diagnosis from their doctor which further underlined the point of the STS programme. When the presentations were finished an open and frank question and answer session was held which possibly had the greatest impact of all. Later reflecting on her role at the event, Samixa Shah emphasised what a great experience it had been and that although she had been nervous about speaking, she was so pleased to be able to use what happened to her in a positive way to help others.

At the time of that first session, Louise Bayne said of the programme "this is an exciting, pioneering programme that Ovacome is offering for free as a practical and positive way of communicating with the doctors and nurses of the future. The programme has been proved to be an effective way of giving information that is retained by putting real women's voices and faces to ovarian cancer. It brings the story of ovarian cancer alive for students rather than relying on a dry textbook".

The positive impact of that inaugural STS event could not have been predicted. Almost immediately Ovacome began to receive requests from other medical and nursing schools to hold similar sessions, and by the winter of 2014 further events had been held in London, Cambridge, Hertfordshire and Birmingham. STS quickly became much more popular and in demand than the charity had ever envisaged with requests coming in from around the UK. An enormous success.

Over the next six months, Roger and Lyn, plus their friends, raised further significant funds for the programme. Lisa's cousin, Joanna Aspray, nominated Ovacome for a charity award scheme run by her employer, Santander, and was delighted to be awarded £5000. Joanna also helped her mother and aunt raise another £750 in a garden party held in June 2014 and Santander generously matched this amount with a further donation. A close family friend, Richard Stock, decided to run the London Marathon, his first ever, in Lisa's memory, to raise money for the charity. Remarkably for someone who had never run a marathon before, he managed to finish the course in just over four hours. Once all his sponsorship money had been collected it amounted to a massive £5000 (later he raised a further £3,000 by running another marathon). Between Joanna, her mum, aunt, and Richard, a further £11,500 had been raised for STS.

Roger personally continued to raise funds for Ovacome by donating speaker's fees he received, for presentations to interested groups of his and Lyn's exploits to Antarctica, New Zealand and Tonga (all those photographs taken during the trips adding vivid detail to his words) and through payments for newspaper articles and photographs. Whatever the opportunity he never failed to raise the subject of Ovacome, the work the charity does and the STS programme. By the early part of the 2020s, the Clark family and their friends had raised in excess of £25,000 for STS, contributing massively to the ongoing running of the programme.

STS was destined to become an essential element of Ovacome's support offering to the medical profession. Over the six years following inception, more than 60 STS session were held, involving approximately 4,000 medical, nursing and other clinical students. Rave reviews of the programme were common with attendees recommending it to colleagues around the country. Comments such as, *"the session made the symptoms far more memorable"; "it is much more effective than a PowerPoint lecture. I will remember it better!"* and *"amazingly informative"* were just some of the words of praise heaped on the programme by the students. STS not only helped to cement the symptoms of ovarian cancer in the minds of students but to introduce signs of the disease that medical text books often failed to mention. Feedback received confirmed that STS could improve students' knowledge of ovarian cancer signs and symptoms, risk factors and referral guidelines by 50 per cent.

Since inception, many Ovacome members have taken part in delivering their personal messages to medical students through the STS programme. The interaction between members and students often had a profound effect as evidenced by the positive and, sometimes, moving dialogue between those present. Shortly before the COVID-19-induced national lockdown in March 2020, Jo Nicholson, a sufferer, volunteer, staff member and overall role model for the charity, held a session at her local GP clinic. One of the GPs in attendance asked Jo, 'What more can we do?'

Jo responded, Listen to us when we come back with symptoms,' and 'When you see a possible case, remember my face.' The GP nodded in agreement. STS had made a difference.

Chapter 7

BOOSTING REPRESENTATION, STYLE AND SERVICES

In late 2004, Ovacome appointed a new chairperson, Noeline Young. Noeline took the chair as an experienced senior nurse who had specialised in cancer services for over ten years and had set up a support group for gynaecological cancer patients in her local area. She also had direct experience of Ovarian cancer as, in 2000, her daughter, Hannah, had been diagnosed with the disease. Eight months later, Noeline personally was diagnosed with borderline ovarian cancer. Noeline remained as chairperson for more than ten years and during her tenure oversaw many developments and improvements in the services, operations and international reach of the charity.

Representation of the charity's members was a priority for Noeline. Given her background and experience, she was very well qualified to work with Louise Bayne, director of the charity, in representing Ovacome members at meetings of many of the nation's influential cancer bodies. Key amongst those were: the National Cancer Research Institute (NCRI), the National Cancer Research

Network (NCRN) the coordinating body for all cancer research, and the National Institute for Clinical Excellence (NICE). At these meetings and conferences Noeline and Louise championed the ovarian cancer patient perspective, often drawing on first-hand knowledge gained from their interactions with individual members of the charity, and the results of member surveys. As in previous years, Ovacome staff continued to attend and present at each of the main political parties' annual conferences. All this work, over many years, plus similar activities with advocacy groups in the UK and abroad, ensured that Ovacome was positioned as the prime representative charity for ovarian cancer support on the national stage.

At a regional level, the question of how best to promote and represent Ovacome's services across the country had been a challenging one almost since set up. To respond to this, the role of regional Ovacome coordinator (ROC) had been introduced in 2003 (see chapter 3), complementing and partly replacing the Fone Friends initiative that had been started within weeks of the charity's establishment. Five years later, the ROC role was enhanced and given a new (even longer!) acronym: ROCC, or regional ovarian cancer coordinator. This was an ambitious, nationwide programme, developed in conjunction with the Eve Appeal charity, funded by a grant from Boots the chemist, and headed up by a new member of staff, Ruth Grigg.

Ruth's job was to provide dedicated support, training and advice to the ROCCs, and her immediate goal was to find and appoint 50 Ovacome members willing to represent the charity at regional level. An apparently daunting task, Ruth quickly discovered the endless enthusiasm and willingness of members to help and achieved more than half of her target within a few weeks. An inaugural training event was organised and held in London in November 2008 where the newly appointed ROCCs spent a day learning about recruiting supporters; the structure of the NHS; writing press releases and running the Fone Friends network before returning home to start their own projects and initiatives based on what they had learned. ROCCs had an immediate impact in their local areas. There was a renewed effort to ensure that Ovacome material was displayed and available in GP surgeries and local hospitals. A display of the Eve Appeal's and Ovacome's work was put up in a Boots store in Portsmouth. The ROCC for Cumbria, Judith Slattery, was interviewed by her local ITV station, talking about the symptoms of ovarian cancer, what to look out for and when to seek medical advice. Four months later, a second training event was held, again in London, for the next group of new recruits and a further event was planned for new ROCCs in the north of England and Scotland.

Over the next four years, the ROCCs rolled with ever increasing success. By the summer of 2011, a total of 42 ROCCs had been recruited, trained, and engaged with their local area. Innovative events were organised and held by ROCCs all over the country: in Welwyn Garden City, Saba Shahdad, a clinical scientist, held an information day at her employer, Roche Pharmaceutical, using BEAT materials to inform her colleagues of the disease; in Croydon, Sue Martensz held a fundraising event at a hotel close to Gatwick airport where she worked; in Southend, Wendy Davies organised a half marathon walk in the dark for herself and friends, supported by the local Rotary club. In Southsea, Dorothy Petty arranged a spectacular 50s-style fancy dress party, based on the musical *Guys and Dolls*; attended by more than 50 friends and supporters she raised more than £1000 for Ovacome. Julie Spokes, the ROCC for Berkshire, had a unique opportunity in April 2011 to get herself in front of TV cameras. Julie lived in Bucklebury, close to the home of Kate Middleton who was about to marry Prince William. To celebrate the event, the village held a party at which Julie was interviewed by *BBC South Today* reading a poem about the newlyweds and wearing, prominently, her Ovacome and Eve Appeal badges.

Several other ROCCs featured prominently on TV, particularly in January 2012 when the potentially very positive impact of the new drug, Avastin, hit the news for the first time. Adele Sewell, Sue Martensz and Helen Cooper, all naturals in front of the camera, did a great job in promoting awareness of the disease with appearances on *Sky News*, ITV's *Breakfast Show*, *ITV Central News* and Voxafrica, amongst others. ROCC stars all!

As mentioned elsewhere in these pages, Ovacome was set up to be, and remains, fundamentally a support charity. Part of that support offer is to ensure that the voice of those who have developed the disease is heard clearly in government circles, and this has been supported over the years by regular surveys of members' needs and concerns. Since the early days of the charity, Ovacome had made representations to government and related bodies on behalf of its members, for example, in 1997, launching a project for the Department of Health, to better understand ovarian cancer patients' needs of their GPs and primary care team.

One big issue that had long been observed was that hospitals across the regions of the UK achieved differing levels of survival rates, access to clinical trials and patient experiences. In the light of these anomalies, in 2011, as the austerity measures introduced, following the financial crisis of 2008/9, bit into NHS budgets, Ovacome decided to mount its biggest parliamentary lobbying campaign to that date. The central part of the initiative was Ovacome writing, in support of its members and gynaecological cancer centres, to each MP, showing them how hospitals in their constituency fared against the national average across key success measures. As important, the charity called on its members to visit the constituency surgery of their MP to discuss the results and stress the importance of them getting involved. Also, it suggested to members that they may wish to visit their local gynaecological oncology team with their MP and to invite local media to report the event. This initiative was a first for an ovarian cancer charity and had been made possible by Ovacome being willing and able to apply the time and resources to collate information available from several reliable sources.

This highly visible initiative was complemented the following year with a parliamentary reception held by Ovacome in Portcullis House, the office building for MPs opposite the Houses of Parliament. At the reception

Ovacome staff presented facts that highlighted the significant differences in treatment, care and patient information provided by hospitals throughout the country. The event was considered to be a big success with 30 MPs, from all the main parties, attending. Subsequently several stories appeared in the local newspapers of the MPs attending, and members of the charity continued to talk to their own MP at their constituency surgeries. Once again, Ovacome supporting its own constituents.

Ovacome's presence on the international stage for ovarian cancer charities had been established in the summer of 2001 when Louise Bayne attended a conference of international ovarian cancer charities in New York (see chapter 2). This had led to an international ovarian cancer forum being established, and 12 years later, a new and ambitious initiative was launched, in which Ovacome and Louise played a key role – the setting up of the inaugural World Ovarian Cancer Day, held on May 8th 2013.

To mark the day that year, Louise, some staff and several members of the charity walked the streets of London taking photographs of the capital and its people which were later added to the charity's social media accounts. These included a picture of the team with David Lammy MP at Westminster, a group of Metropolitan Police officers and a bagpipe player, all holding placards advertising the cause and Ovacome. Globally, 27 ovarian cancer charities, from 17 countries, participated in the event, ensuring that the disease and the work of the charities, was widely publicised. Over the next two years, World Ovarian Cancer Day became established in the calendar of events of many ovarian cancer charities globally. In the UK the four leading charities came together on May 8th 2014, to ask women to pledge to tell five others about the disease. One year later they celebrated the natural bond between women, encouraging them to post photographs of themselves on social media and to sign an awareness pledge.

In 2016 the international campaign for ovarian cancer took the next major step forward with the establishment of the World Ovarian Cancer Coalition. Building on the success of the awareness day initiative, the coalition launched the "Every Woman Study" in 2018 that surveyed more than 1500 sufferers of the disease, across 44 countries, to understand their experiences of ovarian cancer, including diagnosis, treatment, care and information made available. The study, which was guided by an expert advisory panel and 37 clinicians from across the globe, was published in 15 different languages and highlighted significant variations in experiences around the world, confirming (or, perhaps, reconfirming) the need for four key areas of focus globally:

1. The need to raise overall awareness of the disease and its symptoms
2. The importance of family history and access to genetic testing
3. The need for access to specialist treatment and clinical trials
4. The need for access to the support and information patients and their families need

Two years later, largely based on the results of the survey, a global charter was launched, outlining six global goals intended to drive short- and medium-term improvements for those with the disease, no matter where they lived. An international call to action.

World Ovarian Cancer Day remains the flagship global awareness raising event of the coalition. In 2021, the day was supported by almost 200 organisations around the world and was estimated to have reached over 100 million individuals. Since inception of the first awareness day in 2013, Ovacome has been a supporter of the coalition and continues to be one of the founding partner organisations.

Since inception in 1996 Ovacome had utilised a "tree of life" image, together with the word **OVA**COME (OVA in bold typeface) as its presentational style, or logo. As the charity approached the end of its first decade, it was felt that a refresh was needed, and the leadership's thoughts turned to how to achieve this. Fortunately, in 2005, the charity was approached by a well-known design and public relations firm, Coley Porter Bell, who offered to develop a new logo and "look" for the charity on a pro bono basis. Bronwen Edwards and Philip Stevenson of the firm consulted with Ovacome's members to determine what they valued about the charity. During those discussions, terms like "getting information", "emotional support", "personal contact" and "encouragement" were raised frequently, and this led Bronwen and Philip to merge these related needs into the term "dialogue"; dialogue between Ovacome and its members, their families and friends, health professionals, politicians and other third party stakeholders.

Based on their analysis, the tree of life and OVACOME logo was replaced by a cleaner look: OVACOME plus two pink dots. OVACOME.. The dots being there, first to represent ovaries and second, to highlight the charity's purpose to engage in a dialogue with all its stakeholders. This fresh new look was launched by Jenny Agutter, Ovacome's patron, at the members' day event in May 2005. Subsequently, the design of the newsletter and the website were changed to incorporate the new logo and present a fresher look to the user. The logo has stood the test of time and remains in 2021.

Ovacome's factsheets came under scrutiny next. The original documents, produced shortly after set-up, had been improved from time to time, but in 2009 a major initiative was put in place to revamp and update them, with the aim of making them clearer to read and understand. As a result of the work, each of the 15 new factsheets was approved to carry the crystal mark of the "Plain English Campaign", an organisation dedicated to clear and concise information in plain English. The new set covered a broad range of clinical topics, such as types of ovarian cancer; staging; symptoms and treatment options, but also including more intimate subjects such as ovarian cancer-related menopause issues and sexuality. When brought together the factsheets provided a comprehensive overview of many of the significant issues related to an ovarian cancer diagnosis and its subsequent treatment.

Member services, constantly under review by the staff team, took on a new dimension in 2010, thanks to the ever developing capabilities of technology. Working with Health Unlocked, an organisation specialising in technology for health professionals and charities, two important interactive tools were created. The first was titled "My Ovacome" and by clicking on a tab with that name, members and healthcare professionals could sign in to discuss health issues and access information and advice about ovarian cancer. The second, titled "The Big Question", was a monthly poll focused on a "hot topic" with the goal of generating discussion between users and providing important analytics for the charity.

Both proved to be a huge success. The My Ovacome feature provided functionality that included "Inner Circle", a private site for family and friends to communicate; a "Group Blog" and "Helpvine", an online group helpline that allowed members to ask questions of the wider group and/or to respond to previous issues raised. Importantly, My Ovacome provided details of current research and clinical trials, factsheets and lists of other local and national support organisations. Together with the ROCCs programme, these new online features helped to create an even greater sense of community for members, their families and friends and healthcare professionals.

In the same year a new specialised service was established by Ovacome, focusing on younger persons with ovarian cancer. The initiative was driven largely by a young woman, Kerry Briggs, who had developed ovarian cancer at the age of 37. Kerry felt an overwhelming need to speak to others of a similar age in her position but could find little beyond an online forum run by Macmillan Cancer Trust which, whilst helpful for her, did not provide the face to face contact she craved. Kerry turned to Ovacome and spoke with Ruth Payne, one of the charity's support line nurses at the time and, as a result, they jointly launched a physical support group that held its initial meeting in January 2010.

Kerry described the event in the following words: "The meeting was a big success. The turnout exceeded expectations and the group was brimming with enthusiasm and positivity – there was an almost tangible group sigh of relief – to have met others in a similar position and to know that we can move forward in an environment where we will find true understanding, support and form new friendships". Following the event, Ovacome moved swiftly to organise a schedule of future meetings and to provide a dedicated area of the website for younger members suffering from the disease.

At the time, this specialist group was novel, but it provided an early blueprint for the range of specialist groups that Ovacome was to develop over the following ten years. A structure that became invaluable to the charity and its users when the COVID-19 pandemic emerged in 2020 forcing physical meetings to be abandoned.

Chapter 8

ANYONE FOR TEA...
CHAMPAGNE?

If a charity gets lucky, once in every generation, someone comes along who, despite their own challenges, contributes so much to the cause that they become icons within the charity, and sometimes beyond. Ovacome has been extremely lucky to have had several such personalities during its first 25 years of existence, some mentioned in this book. One of their number is the estimable Adele Sewell.

Adele remembers very well the date on which she first became a volunteer for Ovacome – 5th November 2009, the same date as her daughter, Zindzi's, birthday. Zindzi had asked her mother if she would take her and some friends for afternoon tea as a birthday present which Adele was more than happy to do. Visiting a few possible locations for that tea, Adele discovered that the May Fair hotel in Stratton Street, London, had a special offer available, charging £15 per person instead of their usual £20. Adele booked, the ladies attended, and everyone had a wonderful afternoon.

A few months later, in the spring of 2010, Ovacome, together with another gynaecological charity, the Eve Appeal, suggested to members that they hold a tea party at their homes to help raise funds. Adele took this idea a step further and approached the May Fair hotel to see if they would provide afternoon tea to a larger group than her daughter's birthday party and still charge her £15 per person which the hotel's management agreed. Adele's business plan was to charge attendees the full £20, mix in some other fundraising ideas, such as a raffle, and see how much money she could raise. The event (together with many others around the country) was held and raised £450. Adele's employer at the time, Fidelity International, offered a grant scheme to fund match charitable activities of its employees and through that Adele was able to double the amount raised and contribute a total of £900 to Ovacome. She was thrilled and so was the charity.

Flushed with this success, Adele thought that maybe, just maybe, she could repeat the event and attract an even larger audience, the following year. To quote an old English proverb, "mighty oaks from small acorns grow".

Ovacome's heroines and heroes – Adele Sewell's story

Adele Sewell first experienced cancer in 1999 when she was 36 years old, married, with a four year old daughter and living in south London. She had found a lump in her breast and saw her GP, who suspected cancer and referred her to a consultant oncologist. Quite quickly the breast cancer diagnosis was confirmed, and a lumpectomy carried out. The cancer had been discovered at an early stage and Adele's prognosis was good. Radiotherapy and five years' treatment with the drug tamoxifen followed the surgery, and Adele got on with her life and work (she is a graduate physicist).

Eight years later, Adele began to experience a wholly different range of symptoms to those of her previous illness and visited her GP again. Unfortunately, this time, diagnosis would prove to be a far lengthier and more stressful episode. Starting with lower back pain at the beginning of 2006 the symptoms steadily progressed through that year and into 2007. They included sciatica, constipation, pain near her navel and then lower abdomen, changes to urinary habit. Throughout, Adele visited GPs as each new symptom appeared and was sometimes treated for them individually. At one point she left the doctors surgery with two types of laxatives. At no time was a CA125 test or ultrasound scan offered to her; unfortunately, an all too common experience.

Matters came to a head in the summer of 2007. Adele describes what happened next: "I had arranged to join a friend on a short cruise leaving from Florida and met my daughter for lunch shortly before flying to the USA. During lunch I felt unwell and wondered if I should take the cruise or not, deciding eventually that I would. A few days later I flew to New York, a stopover before flying on to Florida and felt so unwell that I called my sister, who is a doctor in America, and talked through my symptoms with her. I then flew to Florida and joined the cruise but felt unwell much of the time. I remember clearly that at the formal dinner evening that most cruises hold at least once during the trip, I had chosen to wear a dress that previously had been quite a loose fit on me. But this time it was very tight around my abdomen, and I felt as if I were pregnant."

Immediately on her return to the UK, Adele arranged an emergency appointment at her local surgery and, this time, saw a different GP who suggested that she may have ovarian cysts and referred her for an ultrasound scan and an appointment with a gynaecological consultant. As part of the consultation a blood test was taken which showed that her CA125 level was over 2000, compared to a normal level of 35 or below. The ultrasound confirmed ovarian cysts, probably some malignant and some not. Ovarian cancer was considered to be highly probable. It had taken 18 months from first symptoms to diagnosis.

Surgery followed and stage 3C high grade serous ovarian cancer was confirmed. Adele commenced the standard chemotherapy regime of carboplatin and paclitaxel and was told that there was a 70%-90% chance that her cancer would recur within two years; prophetic, as, right on schedule, two years later it returned, this time on the surface of her bowel. Further surgery, further chemotherapy, further expectation of another recurrence within two years, or less. But Adele is not a lady to accept simplistic statistics and vowed to continue her life and work. Eight years passed before symptoms returned, in the late summer of 2018, and she had to go back to the doctor. It was at this point that events became a little confusing for Adele and her family. The latest tumour was initially diagnosed as being on her liver and surgery was undertaken in October to remove it. The normal post-surgery consultation was arranged, and Adele was joined by her husband, Tony, both expecting confirmation that the removed tumour was indeed a recurred ovarian malignancy. To their initial elation they were told that the surgery had been successful and that no cancerous tissue had been found. But, immediately tempering their mood, the doctor added that her post-operative CT scan suggested that a tumour still existed. Confusion, devastation. To add to the dejection, the doctor suggested that further surgery would carry too many risks and advised her to avoid it.

Two months later, Adele was chatting with Cathy Hughes, chair of Ovacome and a highly qualified and experienced gynaecological nurse, at the Ovacome Christmas party. After listening to Adele's recent experiences and circumstances, Cathy suggested that she should seek a further opinion from a colleague of hers, Christina Fotopolou, professor of gynaecological oncology at Imperial College London. Adele took Cathy's advice, expecting a confirmation of the opinion she already had, but was surprised and delighted when Professor Fotopoulou agreed to perform a further surgery. That procedure occurred in early February 2019 and discovered that the remaining tumour was located not on the liver but just above the diaphragm. It was successfully removed. Four more months of chemotherapy followed, ending in July 2019. Adele remains in remission.

Following her first diagnosis of ovarian cancer in 2007, Adele had wondered why she had been so unlucky to have developed the disease at all, and only eight years after breast cancer. Her consultant suggested that there may be a genetic link, spoke to her about the BRCA gene mutation (see chapter 1A) and suggested she complete a family history form. Through this she discovered that at least four members of her father's family had died of cancer. It appeared that, if there was a genetic link, it was probably from her dad's side (later, in 2011, Adele's father died of prostate cancer) and Adele decided to have a blood test to check for a BRCA mutation. The result confirmed a mutation of her BRCA 2 gene. Adele realised immediately the probable implications for her family, daughter Zindzi and her two sisters and two brothers, as a parent with a mutated BRCA gene carries a 50% risk of passing that on to their own children. Of her four siblings, two were tested and of those her sister, Yvette, carried the mutation and developed breast cancer in 2008 which was treated successfully. As for Zindzi, as Adele says, it is her decision whether to be tested or not, and no pressure from Mum!

Adele first noticed Ovacome's website in early 2009 and decided to attend the charity's members' day meeting in May that year. That meeting was the first time Adele had met any others with ovarian cancer. A few months later she had joined the ranks of the Fone Friends team and subsequently became one of the charity's regional ovarian cancer coordinators (ROCC).

Following her modest success with "Time for Tea" at the May Fair hotel in 2010, Adele teamed up with fellow ROCC, Sue Martensz, to stage an expanded party at the same hotel in March 2011. Full of enthusiasm and energy, the pair decided that this time, in addition to afternoon tea and a raffle, some champagne and additional events should be added to help attract more attendees and, simply, to add more fun to the event. The idea of holding a fashion show (what could be more fun?) percolated to the surface; plus live music from a guitarist; plus the sale of handmade silver jewellery! But who would be willing to model? Step forward Adele's and Sue's daughters, Zindzi and Gemma, together with a group of their school friends. Adele and Zindzi loaned some of their own clothes for the occasion, supplemented by fashions from the designer, Marcia Green of BeYouT fashion. The scene was set for a great success. Over 100 guests attended, several of them travelling from far reaches of the country to be there and show their support. Once again Fidelity International sponsored the event and, in total, over £5,000 was raised for the charities, Ovacome and the Eve Appeal, both of whom were delighted to say the least.

The 2012 event followed a similar pattern to 2011 but with even more attractions. Jenny Agutter, Ovacome's patron, gave a talk on how members could involve themselves in Ovarian Cancer Awareness Month (OCAM), held in March every year; a red carpet and photographer added extra "sparkle" and the designers, Joanna Hall of Bazaar and Marcia Green of BeYouT, set up stalls. A fashion show was, once again, the highlight of the afternoon but there was one big difference to the previous year, forced by circumstance on Adele and her fellow organisers. That year was "AS" level exam year for Zindzi and her friends and they could not spare the time away from study to be models. As a result, Adele decided to model herself and to invite five other members of the charity who had had cancer to join her; an inspirational idea that was to become the hallmark of future events. The models took to the catwalk to the song 'Survivor' by Destiny's Child, resulting in hardly a dry eye in the house. Attendance increased to a capacity 140 (Adele had a waiting list of others who wanted to attend but space was limited) and over £6000 was raised. Magnificent! It was around this time that Adele realised fully that she had a formula that could be developed and exploited further for the benefit of charity. And so, almost as soon as the table cloths had been cleared, and the tea cups washed and dried in the kitchens of the May Fair hotel, planning for future events began in earnest.

Adele formed a "Tea with Ovacome" committee with the goal of making the annual event part of the ovarian cancer social calendar within five years; Facebook and Twitter accounts were set up. For the 2013 event, capacity was raised to 200 guests but still all tickets were sold, three weeks in advance. David Lammy MP, whose mother had died of ovarian cancer, was confirmed as the keynote speaker and BBC journalist, Helen Fawkes (who wrote a regular column for Ovacome's newsletter about her personal experience of the disease) happily agreed to join other members of the charity, all fellow sufferers or survivors, modelling on the catwalk. Through a contact of one of the members of the Tea with Ovacome committee, Karen McGhie, clothes were loaned for the event by fashion retailer, Apricot; the beginning of an enduring relationship between the two organisations.

The big day, Saturday 16th March, arrived; a cold and drizzly afternoon forecast. But nothing was going to dampen the enthusiasm of this team. The models arrived at the hotel at 11am for a stage rehearsal and music check. By noon the Tea with Ovacome team had all arrived and preparations moved into overdrive. The red carpet was rolled out for arriving guests and a reception desk set up. In the ballroom a transformation was taking place. Hundreds of balloons adorned the space, some tied to the tables and chairs, others floating to the ceiling; teal and turquoise "jewels" were sprinkled across the tables, glittering in the lights like twinkling stars; goody bags filled with treats generously donated by a range of companies were placed by each chair, ready for the eager guests to discover and be thrilled by. At 2pm, Ayanna Witter-Johnson, the well-known cellist, singer and composer, who had agreed to perform at the event, arrived for her sound check. All was ready; the team calm, composed... And electrified!

At 2:15pm, the first guests arrived, 45 minutes ahead of the scheduled start time and soon there was a steady flow of excited members, friends and supporters moving through to the ballroom to be greeted by a champagne reception. Old friends reunited and new friendships formed as guests mingled, chatted, and visited the various stalls that had been set up. Tea was served at 4pm and Ruth Grigg, volunteer and information manager of Ovacome, welcomed everyone to the event. Next, David Lammy spoke movingly of his mother's experience with ovarian cancer and the symptoms to look out for. The rest of the afternoon and evening was given over to the fashion show, an auction of donated items, the raffle and a mesmerising performance by Ayanna Witter-Johnson.

Everyone agreed that the entire programme had been a sparkling success. Well organised, beautifully staged and delightfully carried through. In the process £7,000 was raised for Ovacome. Could it get any better? Well, yes, it could, and it did.

Over the next six years, the Tea with Ovacome (the title evolved to Touch of Teal Tea with Ovacome and then, simply, Touch of Teal) annual event developed into one of the most eagerly anticipated dates in the calendar, with tickets selling out within weeks, if not days, of being announced. Apricot designed a unique dress each year, in the internationally recognised colour for ovarian cancer, teal, which was showcased at each fashion show and then put on sale across their stores and online. Additionally, they designed and produced the annual goody bag, donating all profits from the sale of both dress and bag to Ovacome; an amazingly generous gesture. Very desirable items and experiences were donated for auction by a wide range of individuals and companies, including Philip Treacy, the milliner, who frequently donated a hat in memory of his friend Isabella Blow who had died of ovarian cancer. In addition to Apricot, other fashion designers loaned their creations to the models requiring the number of catwalks to be expanded from one to three. Guests made pledges to raise funds for the charity over the next year and many set up charitable giving pages, leading to even more funds being raised and donated. Hairdressers, beauticians and manicurists all gave their time freely to make sure the models each year had the best possible attention lavished on them.

By the year 2020, planning for the event was a well-established routine and, as usual, had commenced in the autumn of the previous year. By January most of the plans were in place with the recent news of a strange virus appearing on the other side of the world hardly being noticed. Within just a few weeks, that had all changed as the UK and the rest of the world plunged into the reality of COVID-19. Time for Teal 2020, arranged, as always, for March, had to be cancelled. Or did it?

Undeterred, Adele and her team set about making arrangements to hold the event digitally in October. And so it was that Touch of Teal went international on October 3rd, with some 500 participants joining virtually from many countries. As usual a fashion show was held, but this time with the ladies modelling on improvised "catwalks" at their homes. Entertainment was provided in the form of live music and the comedienne, Rosa Hesmondhalgh (AKA Madame Ovary), gave a comedic take on her own ovarian cancer diagnosis. As in previous years, Touch of Teal 2020 had been an inspirational event.

Through her, and her team's, dedication and determination over more than a decade, Adele's original idea to hold a tea for a few friends and supporters had blossomed into an annual event that, by 2020, had raised over £250,000 for Ovacome. Additionally, awareness of ovarian cancer unquestionably had grown through the publicity raised from each event. As important, many of the models, who had experienced the disease, had taken the opportunity to display their personalities and confidence in the face of their illness.

As one of the models from the class of 2018 put it: "Strutting my stuff on the catwalk I was full of emotion, but the atmosphere and support was outstanding. It was so empowering to share the occasion with 12 beautiful, strong women who have now become friends and most importantly I helped raise awareness and essential funds for Ovacome".

In the autumn of 2020 Adele's near heroic efforts led to her being announced as the winner of *Women & Home* magazine's Amazing Women Award 2020 for the south east and south west of England. A truly deserved recognition for a truly exceptional lady.

Chapter 9

OVARIAN CANCER AWARENESS MONTH (OCAM)

In common with other (but not all) charities and causes, ovarian cancer has a designated awareness month which, in the UK, is March. During that month ovarian cancer charities (there are four main charities, including Ovacome, and many smaller ones), launch their own special programmes to raise both awareness of the disease, and funding; helped by the fact that the press and media take a greater interest throughout the month.

OCAM emerged in the middle years of the noughties, modestly at first but gaining traction and attention as the decade progressed. Ovacome, at that time the only national charity specifically for ovarian cancer, became involved immediately, encouraging and supporting members and their families and friends to raise much needed funding through sponsored events and collections. As just one example, in 2005, one member, Debbie Kucha, raised £2400 for Ovacome through a combination of these activities – a wonderful contribution.

Over the next two years, Ovacome teamed up with the Eve Appeal, a charity supporting research into all four gynaecological cancers, to promote fundraising tea parties at members' homes. In 2006 eleven Ovacome members held parties, raising over £3,000. Amongst those was Gill Johnson, an Ovacome member in Cumbria, who decided to base her event around her 41st birthday. Gill invited family and friends who had supported her throughout her own diagnosis and treatment. In addition to the numerous cups of tea drunk and cakes consumed, guests were able to view a scrapbook of Gill's experiences of diagnosis and treatment, plus the support she had received, which she had put together over the past twelve months. Through her efforts Gill raised more than £500 and was so thrilled with the outcome that she repeated the event the following year. Another member, Lynette Wood, added a twist to the tea party idea by deciding to run one from her home over a 12-hour period, inviting people to drop in at any time during the day. In total more than 200 turned up, sampling tea, buying cakes from a stall set up and entering the tombola with prizes donated by local businesses. When added up, all the money received from the day totalled a magnificent £3,200, to be split evenly between Ovacome and the Eve Appeal.

As well as tea parties, other members raised funds through a multitude of events, some of them quite gruelling. Rona Murray, from Oxfordshire, decided to join a 112-kilometre trek across the Sahara Desert, in support of a close friend diagnosed with ovarian cancer. Trekking across a range of terrains, from very stony ground to 300-metre high sand dunes, Rona recalls especially the last day, walking across barren salt flats, in a temperature of 50 degrees Celsius! Through sponsorship, Rona was able to raise over £2,000 for Ovacome. The word awesome would not be an overstatement in her case!

One year later, Ovacome's fundraising efforts during OCAM moved up a gear through the introduction of a targeted campaign. As ovarian cancer was (and still is) often referred to as a silent or hidden disease, the idea was to ask members and their families and friends to find money that had become "hidden" in the home, for example, down the back of a sofa or the side of an armchair, or anywhere. Ovacome provided a small cardboard collecting box, in the shape of a house, for each participant to store the money found during the month. This idea proved to be fun and very popular, especially with children, and was repeated the following year. Naturally, the normal tea parties and other fundraising events, all well established by now, continued and contributed to the many thousands of pounds raised.

OCAM 2009, whilst following a similar pattern to previous years, coincided with the announcement of the preliminary results of the United Kingdom Collaborative Trial of Ovarian Cancer Screening (UKCTOCS) which were encouraging (although eventually were to demonstrate that screening for ovarian cancer did not lead to improved survival – see chapter 3). Together OCAM and UKCTOCS generated substantial media interest and awareness of the disease. Many Ovacome members were interviewed for newspaper and magazine articles, and some appeared on live television, talking about ovarian cancer and the trial results.

If the first five years of Ovacome's endeavours during OCAM had seen a ramping up of activity, the next five were to prove more spectacular. Ovacome's work to find a communication method to embed awareness of ovarian cancer symptoms in the public's memory had resulted in the development of a campaign named BEAT (see chapter 5). BEAT (bloating, eating difficulties, abdominal pain, toilet habits) had been introduced at a press conference in November 2009. But subsequently, a decision was taken to more widely launch the campaign by making it the focus of OCAM the following year. The initiative proved to be a huge success. Members distributed BEAT leaflets and posters to their GP practices; small cards with the BEAT message were produced and handed out at events; Jenny Agutter, Ovacome's patron, made a short video with members of the charity that was posted on YouTube and other media sites. The press response was nothing short of exceptional, giving Ovacome, and the disease, much needed publicity.

Such was the success of combining BEAT with OCAM that it was an obvious decision to continue that over the next few years. The next phase of the BEAT campaign saw the introduction of "Teal Tips", a promotion of a teal (the recognised colour for ovarian cancer) nail varnish produced by the leading polish brand, OPI. Launched by Jenny Agutter in 2011, who was photographed wearing the varnish, several well-known figures joined in over the next three years (OPI was replaced by Barry M in 2013), including Carol Vorderman, Terri Dwyer and Sam Siddall; all with relatives or friends who had developed the disease. Equally important, many of Ovacome's members wore the varnish at awareness and fundraising events around the UK. Beauty bloggers, women's magazines and local press all wrote about Teal Tips, interviewing members wearing the varnish. BBC Radio Solent staged interviews over an entire week, including with Louise Bayne and Noeline Young, Ovacome's chief executive and chair respectively. All helping to raise awareness.

For 2014, the Teal Tips campaign for OCAM expanded to products beyond nail varnish. Apricot, the fashion retailer that had become involved with the "Tea with Ovacome" event (see chapter 8), designed a teal-coloured dress and a matching shopper bag, donating a substantial amount from the sale of each to Ovacome. Teal-themed jewellery, including bracelets and a pair of crystal earrings by Swarovski, were produced and sold. And, of course, another new tint of teal-themed nail varnish, this time named "Teal Tips" was manufactured and sold. All of these sales contributed funds to the charity and the related events raised awareness across the UK.

Over the next three years, Ovacome's programme for OCAM continued the theme established by the previous five but added a fresh new dimension to each. In 2015 the charity launched its "Tell Your Daughter" campaign as its main feature for OCAM. Members were asked to post a selfie of themselves with their daughter on social media, pledging to discuss the symptoms of the disease with her and donating £2 before asking another mother/ daughter pair to do the same. Celebrities, including the former politician Edwina Currie, TV presenter Lorraine Kelly and former Liberty X singer Michelle Heaton, helped the campaign take off. Michelle, who had publicly stated that she had the mutated BRCA 2 gene which gave her a higher risk of developing breast and/or ovarian cancer, and had undergone preventative surgery, said at the time: "Having the BRCA gene has made it even more important for me to tell my daughter Faith about ovarian cancer when she is old enough. But regardless of whether women have this genetic link to the disease or not, they need to tell their daughters about the warning signs, so they know what to look out for before it is too late". Wise words indeed.

The campaign, once again, garnered significant media interest. Both Edwina Currie and Michelle Heaton appeared on TV shows. Popular newspapers and magazines picked up on the celebrity stories and Michelle blogged about many aspects of Ovacome's awareness and fundraising activities in her *OK!* blogs. At the local level, many newspapers interviewed Ovacome members and published their stories. An overwhelming success. The following year Teal Tips went international as Tara Palmer-Tomkinson, a supporter of Ovacome, was photographed for *Hello* magazine on the ski slopes of Klosters wearing that year's teal-themed nail varnish. Jenny Agutter got in on the act by posting a photograph of herself on holiday in Tobago, also wearing the varnish. Other celebrities, including Edwin Currie and Michelle Heaton, once again aided the cause by being seen publicly, and talking about awareness, sporting teal-coloured nails.

For 2017, Barry M teamed with Ovacome to produce party kits for manicure fundraising events. The kit, neatly packaged in a Barry M "mani" bag, contained the Teal

Tips varnish, a cuticle oil, a basecoat and topcoat, a nail file and a corrector pen. The bags also contained Ovacome's BEAT awareness material for members to hand out at each event. Ovacome offered to provide the kit free to the first 20 members who committed to raise at least £50 at their event. They were claimed very quickly!

The next leap for Ovacome's OCAM efforts, in emphasis and ambition, occurred in 2018. With the charity under new leadership (see chapter 10), every day of March that year was designated as an awareness and fundraising day and a target of £55,000 raised from activities throughout the month was set. To say that the target was ambitious would have been a bit of an understatement, but the funds were needed to expand Ovacome's support service provision, particularly a brand new initiative named "Ova to You". The big idea behind Ova to You was to take the charity's physical presence to more towns and cities across the UK, raising awareness, providing support to members directly, and seeking their opinions on matters relating to ovarian cancer and Ovacome.

Throughout the month, Ovacome's website and social media pages displayed a virtual thermometer tracking progress towards the overall target that each week's activities had achieved. Creative fundraising events were held up and down the country: hand-sewn pieces sold in Sunderland; donations for carvery dinners sold in a pub in Spalding; coffee mornings in Leeds; quiz nights in London and many, many more. By the end of an exhausting but hugely satisfying month the total exceeded everyone's hopes, reaching almost £56,000. This huge sum funded Ovacome to hold a Wellbeing Members Day in September and ensured that the charity could pledge to run an Ova to You support day in a different town or city every month.

Headlining the publicity push that year was the "Have you been tealed?" campaign, led, once again, by Jenny Agutter, supported by ten other celebrities including Jane Asher, Nigel Havers, Sara Cox and David Lammy. Each of the celebrities was photographed by professional photographer, Ming Yeung, husband of Ovacome member, Rebecca Readshaw, who had been diagnosed with ovarian cancer more than a year after she first reported symptoms to her doctor. The photographs appeared in a wide range of publications, from the *Sunday Mirror* to *Oncology News*, with the title of the campaign hopefully prompting women to think about the symptoms of the disease.

Following the enormous success of the 2018 campaign, and wishing to be realistic, the following year Ovacome set the same target (£55,000) for fundraising during OCAM. But the commitment and energy of its members once again surprised and thrilled. As usual, a wide range of events was held across the UK, raising funds and awareness. But additionally for 2019, a new idea was introduced: the virtual walk. Simple in concept the goal was to see if members, family, friends, could collectively cover as many steps walking in their homes as it would take to walk the entire length of the shoreline of the British Isles. To help participants log their steps a monitoring wrist band was made available at a cost of £25, or free to anyone who pledged to raise at least £150 through sponsorship. Whilst the challenge commenced in

March, to coincide with OCAM, it could be continued into future months, together with the sponsorship gained. The overall results of all events combined was phenomenal, with a total in excess of £68,000 raised throughout the month, and publicity of Ovacome and the disease spread widely across the UK.

And so, to 2020. As the new year crept over all our thresholds, plans were well advanced for OCAM that March. An overall target to raise £65,000 was set, the virtual walk was to be continued and, once again, a full month of member events was evolving. And then the pandemic hit and just about everything in all our lives, and that of Ovacome, changed. But Ovacome's OCAM work would continue.

Since 2005 Ovacome's commitment to and support of OCAM has developed and grown beyond all measure. From humble beginnings OCAM has become a key focus for all ovarian cancer charities, and certainly for Ovacome. Over a 16-year period, OCAM has brought much to Ovacome – and Ovacome has brought much to OCAM.

Chapter 10

RENEWAL AND CELEBRATION

In the spring of 2013, in the normal course of events, Ovacome appointed a new trustee, Cathy Hughes. Cathy, a highly qualified and experienced gynaecological cancer nurse, had been encouraged to join by Noeline Young, Ovacome's chairperson at that time. Noeline and Cathy knew each other well as they were colleagues at Macmillan Cancer Support. One year later, Noeline, who had been chairperson for more than ten years, decided to step down and Cathy stood, successfully, to replace her in that role. The transition occurred in May 2014.

As Noeline looked back over her ten-year tenure, she was keen to highlight some events and initiatives that stood out in her memory. They included: the agreement of the consensus statement on the symptoms of ovarian cancer that had led to the highly successful BEAT campaign, the development of a fresh and contemporary new logo and look for the charity, the photographic exhibitions that demonstrated just how much celebrity support Ovacome had, the transformation of the newsletter from a simple black and white publication to a glossy, well-edited magazine, the introduction of the Survivors Teaching Students programme and the provision, since the very early days of the charity, of a nurse-led telephone support line; unique to Ovacome at the time of her retirement from the chairpersons role. She also paid tribute to the advances in Ovacome's clinical knowledge and experience, and the role played by the medical board which had ensured that the charity was highly respected and regarded within both the medical community, and the political sphere. Unquestionably, Noeline had helped steer the charity through a period of substantial growth and positive change and vacated the chair with much to be proud of.

The first initiative that Cathy had to oversee was the completion of Ovacome's transition from an unincorporated charity to a charitable incorporated organisation (CIO), a relatively new legal structure at that time. This change had been approved by members at the annual general meeting held in May, the same meeting that had approved Cathy's role as chairperson. Becoming a CIO gave Ovacome several advantages. First, as a CIO, Ovacome could hold property directly (should it so choose), rather than having to do so through appointed trustees. Second, it gave the charity extra credibility with potential funders and other third parties. Thirdly, it provided significant protection against personal liability for the trustees, making it easier to attract high quality candidates. At the same time the change in legal status made very little practical difference to members and other users of Ovacome, as all the assets and capabilities of the old charity transferred to the new. The change was finalised the following year.

A few months later, the trustees of the charity, after some deliberation, took a decision to become involved in funding research into specific aspects of ovarian cancer for the first time. This opportunity arose due to a significant donation by a patient of Ovacome's medical board director, Sean Kehoe. Sean was leading a team of researchers at Birmingham University that was working to understand how tumours changed when they were treated, including the pathways that the malignancy took. The objective was to find new and better treatments for patients, based on the findings of the research. As part of the funding arrangement, Ovacome was to be recognised in any papers published and acknowledged in talks and lectures given by Sean.

Whilst the initiative was an addition to Ovacome's fundamental goal of being a support charity, the circumstances were unusual, and the collaboration created a win-win result for both the charity and medical research. It remains the only research funding that the charity has been directly involved in, although, more recently, Ovacome has collaborated with many other charities that have an interest in ovarian cancer, its causes and treatments. Of particular note, Ovacome has partnered with Ovarian Cancer Action, a charity that does excellent work in helping to fund research into the prevention, diagnosis and treatment of ovarian cancer, to support each other's initiatives.

During the first three years of Cathy's tenure as chairperson, Louise Bayne continued as CEO of Ovacome, and throughout that period Louise and other staff continued efforts to raise understanding of ovarian cancer and what more could be done to help those impacted by the disease. More specifically, those efforts included raising the issue of the authorisation of new drug treatments made available under the NHS. Two such drugs were bevacizumab (marketed as Avastin), a monoclonal antibody (see chapter 4-A), and olaparib, a drug particularly for patients with the BRCA gene mutation.

Avastin, first available in 2010, had been the subject of considerable debate relating to its use and effectiveness. It had been approved by the European Medicines Agency in 2012 and became available in England the same year through the Cancer Drugs Fund (CDF), for both first occurrence and relapsed disease. But at the end of 2014 the CDF removed its funding for recurrent disease, basing its decision on more recent trial results. Ovacome, on behalf of its members, challenged this decision, making representations at many levels, including to the prime minister, David Cameron. At the time, Louise said, "Whilst Ovacome understands the financial challenges facing the NHS and the issues of drug costs, we believe that the current appraisal system is not fit for purpose and needs urgent reform." Subsequently, Ovacome worked with other organisations and the pharmaceutical industry to understand how improvements could be achieved so that women contracting the disease could access the latest treatments.

Olaparib first hit the headlines in the UK as a potentially effective treatment for ovarian cancer in 2014. The drug was the first of the PARP inhibitors (see chapter 11-A) to reach clinical use and was the subject of phase III clinical trials in the summer of 2014. A few months later, the European Commission gave marketing authorisation for the drug but, in the UK, the CDF declined to follow suit, causing some consternation within the medical profession. Ovacome highlighted these events and campaigned for access to the treatment, along with other organisations. Finally, in late 2015, olaparib was approved by the re-named National Institute for Health and Care Excellence (NICE) for treating patients with the BRCA mutation and recurrent disease, who had responded positively to previous platinum based treatment.

Hopefully, the campaigning work of Ovacome (and other charities and organisations) had influenced directly the outcomes of the approval process for these, and other novel treatments. As a minimum they helped raise awareness of the treatment issues, and opportunities to improve outcomes for people living with the disease. Cathy, Noeline and Louise's respective direct representation on several of the UK's key cancer treatment decision-making bodies also made a decisive impact.

"Celebrate with Ovacome at our 20th Birthday Party". That was the call to members and supporters of the charity in the summer of 2016. To mark this historic occasion and celebrate the success of Ovacome, it was decided to replicate the cycle event held to launch the charity in September 1996, but to add a few refinements. The cycle course chosen ran from Richmond Green (Kensington Gardens in 1996) to Alexandra Park, Windsor, the same destination as 20 years previously. To broaden the appeal of the ride, three routes were set out, covering 29, 37 or 55 miles and each rider was free to pick which they would follow. The 29-mile course was designed for those who were of reasonable fitness, as the terrain, which followed some towpaths, was reasonably flat. The 37- and 55-mile routes were intended for more experienced cyclists. Recognising the increased attention paid to safety since 1996, all riders were encouraged to wear helmets. For those who either did not own a bicycle, or could not transport theirs from home, hire cycles were made available from a shop close to the starting point. Not having an available bicycle was no excuse not to participate! Naturally, and in keeping with the original launch event, entertainment, refreshments (including a beer tent!) and music were all provided in the park. For this event a sports massage facility was added, a welcome addition for many riders.

All intending participants were asked to contact the charity in advance to register their planned involvement and pay a nominal entrance fee (to pay the event's organiser). Each rider was sent an Ovacome T-shirt to wear and was encouraged to obtain sponsorship, although this was not mandatory.

Unlike the original event 20 years previously, the weather on the day, September 4th 2016, was not kind, with overcast skies and some rain. Undeterred, the cyclists braved the weather, a runaway bike wheel, failed brakes and the mischievous actions of youngsters who had turned around some of the route signs! On arrival at Alexandra Park, exhausted (and not so exhausted) cyclists were joined by Cathy Hughes, Louise Bayne, other members of staff, families, friends and celebrity supporters. Recognition, celebration and fun for all. Sarah Dickinson, Ovacome's founder, would have been proud.

In another recognition of its 20th anniversary, the charity launched a member survey, the first in ten years, in part to determine how the experience of those who had developed the disease had changed over that period. In total over 400 members completed the survey, answering 61 questions, considerably more than the previous study. One factor that surprised Ovacome's leadership was that persistent bloating, a key indicator of possible disease, did not register as a symptom most likely to lead a women to visit her GP. Also concerning was the finding that the time between the first medical visit and investigation at a hospital had increased from an average of 11.5 weeks, to 19.6 over the ten-year period. On a more positive note, the survey indicated that those worried about personal symptoms were visiting their GP sooner; in less than 10 weeks compared to 29, ten years earlier.

Access to clinical trials was a further issue raised through the survey responses. They demonstrated that only 28% of those diagnosed with the disease were informed of and given the option to consider a clinical trial, although over 70% of those who were offered decided to proceed. This finding made the very recent introduction of Ovacome's first online clinical trial finder tool even more relevant than perhaps had been realised.

The results of the survey were revealed at the members' day meeting in March 2017 and were the subject of much discussion amongst attendees. Additionally, they helped inform Ovacome's future awareness raising campaigns, including at the British Gynaecological Cancer Society's conference held in the summer that year where the subject of bloating as a key symptom was at the forefront of the charity's presentations. A fitting contribution to Ovacome's anniversary year.

Chapter 11

CHANGE AT THE TOP

As 2017 moved into autumn, a change at the top of the charity loomed. Louise Bayne, involved with Ovacome for 20 years – five of those as chairperson, followed by ten as inaugural director/CEO – announced that she was emigrating to New Zealand as her (surgeon) husband had been appointed to a new post there. For the first time in its history, Ovacome was faced with the question of how best to replace the CEO. Cathy Hughes and the trustee board deliberated. Louise had been appointed from within the initial member group of the charity and was employed on a part-time basis. The key question now was: is this the right time to recruit a full time CEO with strong and relevant experience and track record in third sector organisation management, or look inside the charity once again? The decision was taken to pursue the first of those options and a recruitment campaign was put in place with several of the trustees making up a selection panel. Advertisements for the role were placed and candidates duly invited to be interviewed by the panel. Following a rigorous process, completed by the winter, Ovacome had found and appointed its chosen successor to Louise: Victoria Clare.

Victoria was not a total stranger to ovarian cancer. Five years prior to her appointment, she had contacted and received support from Ovacome as she had been diagnosed with an ovarian tumour. Fortunately, in Victoria's case, it proved to be benign, and she was able to continue her work and life. Immediately prior to joining Ovacome, Victoria had been director of a surgical charity working in Ethiopia and CEO of a small, UK-based, head and neck cancer charity. Her work in Ethiopia was often challenging, sometimes in the extreme, due to the conditions on the ground, and she had to develop innovative means of communicating with and supporting the mostly children and young adults that the charity catered for. These skills and experiences were to stand her, and Ovacome, in good stead when pandemic hit the UK and the world in 2020.

Victoria was attracted to Ovacome not only by her personal brush with the disease but by what she saw as the opportunity to develop the charity and take it to the next level. As she said shortly after her appointment, "In all my previous jobs I have grown the reach of the charities or organisations I have worked for and I definitely want to do the same here. The charity has a great message, fantastic experts and a wonderful group of engaged staff, trustees and volunteers. I want to make sure we support as many women (and family members) as we can, at the right time and in the right way." The stage was set.

Victoria immediately discussed with the charity's staff (there were just four at the time) their thoughts about the existing status of Ovacome and their priorities for the future. She took time to speak with the CEOs of other charities focused on gynaecological cancers, to better understand what each was doing and how they could improve communication and coordination with each other. And she decided to launch a new consultation with members in a bid to understand their needs of the charity and how well those were being met.

Whilst this work was proceeding a new initiative, "Ova to You", previously planned, was moving forward. Ova to You was a programme of Ovacome staff going out to meet members at locations across the UK to discuss their experiences of all aspects of ovarian cancer and to hear their views on how Ovacome could improve its services. Amongst the first of such meetings were two held in Bath and Bristol. They proved to be big wake-up calls. Immediately prior to the sessions, Ovacome staff met with cancer nurse specialists at some of the local hospitals. When the feedback from those discussions was added to the information gathered at the member meetings, a picture of widely varying quality of care between that experienced at the major cancer centres (especially in London) and elsewhere, became very clear indeed. At the same time, whilst much of Ovacome's work was lauded, particularly in raising awareness of the disease, members at the regional meetings believed that the charity was too London-centric, and the support services provided were not as consistent as they needed to be. These views were further backed up by the results of the member consultation. It became clear to the leadership that Ovacome had to do more to enhance member (plus family and friends) support activities and to do that more evenly across the country.

Up to that point, Ovacome's direct presence beyond the capital had relied largely on what was, in effect, an outreach programme for members, driven first by Fone Friends, followed by regional Ovacome coordinators (ROCs) and finally regional ovarian cancer coordinators (ROCCs). Each of these programmes had achieved good success and helped many thousands of people deal with the impact of the disease. But each relied on volunteers in local areas and, increasingly, had tended to focus on awareness-raising rather than individual support. By early 2018, the ROCCs programme had largely run its course. It was time for a rethink of how support services should be provided.

Fortunately, Ovacome's fundraising efforts during Ovarian Cancer Awareness Month (OCAM), in March of that year, exceeded expectations and provided a financial base to expand services in a very direct way. Telephone support line services were expanded, and one-to-one direct support sessions were introduced. These actions alone gave users of the charity's services more flexible access and increased personal attention. A members' day had been held annually since Ovacome had been established, but now a second annual day was introduced, focused on health and wellbeing, the format to include presentations, workshops and relaxation classes. It was confirmed that the Ova to You programme would meet at a centre outside of London once a month, the northern cities of Liverpool and Leeds being chosen as the locations for the August and September meetings respectively.

Recognising that ovarian cancer was, increasingly, being stratified into subgroups, and that people of all ages and ethnicities were affected by the disease, Ovacome began to introduce new, more focused, support groups for members (and their families and friends) to join. Local general support groups, many spawned by the ROCC programme, were already in place in over 40 locations across the country, and a group specifically for younger people (less than 45 years old) impacted by the disease had been in place for more than seven years. This group met once a month at a Maggie's centre in Hammersmith, London (Maggie's support centres can be found at many hospitals across Great Britain) and had proved to be popular. The next group established (perhaps inspired by the success of Gareth Malone's popular TV series) was the Ovacome Choir, launched in October 2018 with the celebrated choir leader and conductor, Naveen Arles, as its musical director. Hot on the heels of the choir, another group, open to all women diagnosed with ovarian cancer, was launched in early 2019. But this was just the beginning. Over the next three years, based on feedback from members (including from a new member survey held in 2020), many new groups that met weekly or monthly (virtually during the pandemic), were established. These included fitness classes, yoga, a friends and family group and a simple Friday afternoon chat session. Each of the sessions held helped to provide information, relaxation, or both, but additionally provided a forum for participants to discuss informally just about anything they wished to. In addition to the regular group meetings, Ovacome introduced one-off workshops and discussions covering a broad range of topics from dealing with anxiety to embroidery. Many bonds and friendships have been built through all these activities.

In the summer of 2020, a specialist support group was introduced for those who, as a result of their disease, had been fitted with a stoma (a bag that collects waste directly from either the digestive or urinary tracts). The group was the brainchild of a member of the charity, Jo Nicholson, who had been on the staff many years previously. She went on to co-lead the group, together with one of Ovacome's staff.

Ovacome's heroines and heroes – Jo Nicholson's story

Jo Nicholson first encountered ovarian cancer in the summer of 1997, when she was 32 years old. Jo had been undergoing fertility treatment and, during that process, an ovarian cyst was discovered. A consultation in the autumn was followed by tests and Jo was told that pre-cancerous cells had been discovered. At that point her consultant wanted Jo to undergo radical surgery that, as normal for such surgery, would have led to her not being able to have her own children. Jo decided against that approach and opted for the diseased ovary to be removed. The surgery went ahead and stage 1A ovarian cancer was confirmed. Agonisingly, Jo now faced the dilemma of whether to continue with her fertility treatment in the hope that she could become pregnant prior to further surgery, or to go ahead with the operation immediately.

In common with so many people impacted by the disease, Jo felt alone and wanted to speak to others, particularly those of her age, about their experiences and how they had coped. Fortunately, Jo read about and then contacted Ovacome; a contact that was, as she put it, "going to fundamentally change my life". Jo had several conversations with Louise Bayne and Ruth Payne (support nurse at the time) who raised the possibility of her obtaining a second opinion regarding her medical options. She also chatted with Debbie Howells, a staff member of the charity, who had been through a similar situation and was more than willing to help and share her experiences. Following these discussions, Jo arranged an appointment with Professor Ian Jacobs (see chapter 3) and, ultimately, decided to continue with the fertility treatment.

Shortly after that meeting, Jo offered to help Ovacome on a voluntary basis and became one of the growing group of Fone Friends, a role that she fulfilled for about one year. Whilst she found some of the telephone conversations emotionally difficult, she felt that she was able to help particularly younger persons with the disease, some dealing with similar challenges to her own. Attending another Ovacome members' meeting, Jo once again got chatting with Louise Bayne, resulting in her joining the staff of the charity on a part-time basis. Over the next three years, Jo helped prepare factsheets for the charity, answered the telephone and helped out with any other administrative task that needed doing.

And then, joy of joy, in 2002, Jo fell pregnant, giving birth to a son later that year. Jo turned her attention to bringing up her infant son but remained in touch with Ovacome and, from time to time, helped out with arrangements for the annual members' day. Five years after giving birth, Jo went ahead with preventative surgery to remove her uterus and remaining ovary. All went well and no further malignancy was discovered.

Life continued as normal for the next ten years until, in 2017, feeling unwell, Jo had a consultation and CT scan that showed that cancer had returned. Although ovarian cancer, it had metastasised to her diaphragm. Whilst the news was devastating, Jo was determined to continue her life and, like so many others, do everything possible to combat this latest setback. Further surgery (including at one point the fitting of a stoma) and chemotherapy followed, and Jo responded well. Once again she contacted Ovacome, receiving both support and the latest information available from the charity, whilst offering to help other members in any way she could. Soon Jo had become a regular attendee of Ovacome's support groups, including the choir, arts and crafts and Friday afternoon chat group, and led the stoma group with her irrepressible enthusiasm and good nature.

Wanting to do more, she agreed to become a speaker at Ovacome's Survivors Teaching Students events (see chapter 6). Jo loved these meetings with student medical professionals, particularly the question and answer sessions where she was sure to provide answers in a very frank, personal and intimate way. Immediately prior to the first pandemic-induced lockdown of 2020, Jo presented to a group of GPs at her local practice. In her closing comments she urged them to "remember her face" whenever they saw another woman with symptoms that could suggest ovarian cancer.

But Jo wanted to go one step further; to gain more recognition for Ovacome's work and to thank the charity for the support that had been given to her and her family. In the summer of 2021, she nominated Ovacome for the

Radio 4 All in the Mind award. An annual event, in 2021 the competition received over 1,100 nominations from across the UK. To the delight of all involved with the charity, Ovacome was named as one of only three organisations to reach the final. The final judging and awards ceremony was recorded in early June, to be broadcast on the 30th of that month and Jo and Ovacome's head of support services, Anna Hudson, were invited to attend. Unfortunately, one week before the recording, Jo's health deteriorated, and she was admitted to hospital to stabilise her condition. It seemed that she would not be able to get to the recording after all, a great disappointment for her. But Jo's oncologist had other plans and agreed that she could attend as long as she returned to her hospital bed immediately after. The deal was struck and Jo's husband, Simon, was called on to bring clothing, wheelchair, make up and "pumpkin" chariot (car). As she was wheeled out of the ward to be driven to the ceremony another patient called across "you will go to the ball, Cinderella". And so it was. Jo was able to stand and be interviewed at the event, accompanied and supported by Anna before being whisked back to hospital. Ovacome did not win the award that day, but as Jo said, "every one of the three finalists was a winner". Never a truer word.

Jo died in September 2021.

Over a 24-year period Jo had been both a beneficiary of Ovacome' services and dedication to its members, and an important contributor to much of the good that the charity does. She had written and published, together with her mother and a friend, a frank and deeply personal

book about managing a cancer diagnosis, titled 44 ½
Choices You Can Make if You Have Cancer *and she
played a valuable role in the writing of this book. She
was a great friend of the charity and, as for all members
who have succumbed to the disease, is sadly missed.*

By the spring of 2019, the Ova to You programme and
the newly established support groups were in full flight,
the former having run 20 events across 12 different cities
in an 18-month period. But one major objective,
highlighted by the consultation process and Ova to You
sessions, had not been achieved: taking Ovacome's
physical presence to locations beyond London. To help
reach this goal the charity needed to find specific funds
for that purpose and decided to apply for a National
Lottery People's Projects grant. The People's Project
scheme gave organisations, including charities, the
chance to apply online for funding, up to a maximum of
£50,000, to support initiatives in local communities. In
total £3 million was available through the programme.
Once applications had been received, they were evaluated,
and a shortlist drawn up which was then put to a vote in
the local community that would benefit. Hence, local
residents got to choose their favourite project. In 2019
Ovacome was shortlisted, together with four other
applicants. All fingers and toes were crossed as the results
came through and everyone connected with Ovacome
was thrilled to learn that the charity had won and been
awarded £49,420 to establish a satellite support base in
Birmingham. A little later, at the National Lottery cheque
presentation ceremony, Victoria Clare spoke from the
heart: "This is a huge success and an immense step
towards ensuring that those affected by ovarian cancer

across the UK have access to expert information and specialised support." She went on to say, "We cannot thank each and every one of you enough who gave us your vote and helped to make our ambition of giving even greater support to women in the Midlands a reality. This money will enable us to create a space for those affected by the disease to share experiences and offer each other encouragement, friendship knowledge and understanding."

The Midlands office opened in Dudley in September 2019 and employed its first regional hub co-ordinator. Ovacome had begun its physical expansion into the regions of the UK.

Chapter 11A

DIAGNOSTICS AND TREATMENTS – A BRIEF HISTORY, 2010-2021

Diagnosis:

It is a sad reflection of the difficulties faced in diagnosing ovarian cancer that, once again, little if any fundamental improvement was made in the second decade of the 21St century. General screening had been shown to be ineffective in improving outcomes for those diagnosed with the disease and measuring levels of CA125 through blood tests, ultrasound scanning and biopsy remained the prevalent techniques. However, there is new hope in 2021 as novel techniques that look for changes to DNA that may point to ovarian cancer, are being researched. These are outlined in chapter 14.

Treatment:

From a treatment point of view, the most important advance for many cancers, including ovarian, was the very exciting and promising discovery and introduction of targeted drugs. Put simply, chemotherapy drugs attack cancer cells, causing them to die but, unfortunately, they also kill some healthy cells during the treatment, often leading to unpleasant side effects. Targeted drugs home in on the cancer cells, blocking or inhibiting specific biological features of those cells that enable them to replicate and grow.

One of the most exciting of the class of targeted therapies was the" poly (ADP-ribose) polymerase", or, simply, "PARP" inhibitors; and the first of those to be introduced, in 2014, to treat ovarian cancer was olaparib. Cancer cells have damaged DNA and PARP is an enzyme that they need to repair that damage. Inhibiting PARP can lead to the death of the cancer cells. A phase III clinical trial, titled SOLO 1, demonstrated that the use of olaparib as a maintenance therapy, following surgery and regular chemotherapy, significantly extended the survival time for those patients who carried a BRCA 1/2 gene mutation. Initially, olaparib was approved for use in the UK only for patients who had suffered a recurrence of their cancer. However, in 2019 new approval was issued that ensured that the treatment was available, as a maintenance therapy, from onset of the disease.

Whilst olaparib was the first of the PARP inhibitors effective against ovarian cancer, it was quite swiftly followed by others, including niraparib and rucaparib. An important feature of these two later drugs was that they were effective regardless of whether the patient carried a BRCA 1/ 2 gene mutation or not. Niraparib was approved for use by the NHS in the spring of 2018 and rucaparib in the winter of 2019. Together these drugs opened a new and exciting treatment channel that demonstrated longer overall survival times for many women with the disease.

Further research (ongoing in late 2021) suggested that a combination of olaparib and Avastin (a monoclonal antibody – see chapter 4A) can be even more effective in preventing, or at least slowing down, the progression of disease. In recognition of this advance, NICE approved the use of this combination (through the cancer drugs fund) for those who had a BRCA 1/2 gene mutation or other associated gene alterations, known as homologous recombination deficiency (HRD). As about 50% of women who contract ovarian cancer have HRD, a sizeable population may be helped by this combination therapy.

Further trials of combinations of drugs that inhibit various aspects of cancer cells' ability to repair themselves and grow are showing encouraging results in the early 2020s. It looks as if these targeted, gene level, therapies are opening up new hope for ovarian cancer sufferers.

Significant improvements in drug therapies represented one facet of the overall progress made in treatment during the second decade of the 21st century. But surgical techniques and procedures were another, including attempting to answer the question of whether secondary surgery following a recurrence of ovarian cancer was beneficial or not in prolonging overall survival. A major trial focused on this question, titled "Desktop III" had commenced in 2010 and ran until 2014, involving 80 hospitals across 12 countries, with final results being presented in 2020.

Whilst this trial was in progress, current Ovacome trustee, Lesley Sage, had to make her own decision whether to undergo secondary surgery or not. It was a difficult choice for Lesley and her family.

Lesley, from Moulton, near Spalding in Lincolnshire first became aware of a potential gynaecological problem in 2011. She booked a cervical smear at her GP surgery (which identified no problems; cervical smears do not identify ovarian cancer), told the nurse about some bleeding and asked her to feel a lump in her lower abdomen. Fortunately for Lesley, her GP practice had a policy at that time that any post-menopausal patient who reported her type of symptoms was seen by a doctor before they left the surgery. Her doctor completed an examination and was unhappy with the result.

A few days later Lesley had a consultation with a gynaecological oncologist followed by a CT scan which suggested cancer in one ovary and at least one lymph node. A hysterectomy was performed, with removal of the ovaries and lymph node; follow up pathology tests confirmed (relatively rare) stage 3 clear cell ovarian cancer. Chemotherapy followed using the well-established carboplatin and paclitaxel combination. Unfortunately, 18 months later, Lesley suffered further symptoms and went back to her oncologist.

More tests and scans revealed that the cancer had re-established very close to two main blood vessels, the aorta and the renal artery, and in the opinion of her oncologist, Lesley's best course of action was to restart chemotherapy immediately as further surgery was out of the question due to the high risks involved. Lesley turned to her daughter, Beth, who, at that time, was a hospital registrar specialising in respiratory medicine and was also close to completing a PhD in stem cell treatments. Beth was aware of a team based at Imperial College Hospital, London, that was building a reputation for carrying out surgery in very difficult cases of gynaecological cancers. That team was led by Alan Farthing, a surgeon gynaecologist to the royal household, and included senior surgeon Professor Christina Fotopoulou. Alan and his team agreed to review Lesley's medical history and confirmed that, in their opinion, a second operation, whilst difficult, could be undertaken successfully and that in their view it was in her best interest to take that path. Lesley felt immediately that it was the right thing to do and, after some discussion, her family agreed. Secondary surgery would go ahead.

The date for the operation was set for about two weeks later, on Valentine's Day, February 14th 2013. Lesley and her husband, Pat, travelled to London the previous evening, ready for admission to the hospital at 7:30am the following morning. Lesley was duly delivered to hospital and Beth and Adam took Pat shopping for his first iPhone as a distraction! The surgery, carried out by Christina Fotopoulou, together with Alan Farthing, lasted over two hours and was a big success. All the abnormal lymph node tissue that had attached to Lesley's aorta and renal artery was removed with the loss of just 200ml of blood and no need for intensive care post operation. Adam Farthing was delighted to telephone Pat and relay the good news. Four weeks later Lesley started dose dense chemotherapy, once again with carboplatin and paclitaxel but this time with the addition of 12 cycles of Avastin. Lesley remains free of ovarian cancer in early 2022.

Lesley is always keen to point out that secondary surgery, followed by chemotherapy, is not appropriate in every case of relapsed ovarian cancer. Certain criteria and medical history have to be observed and met if a successful outcome is to have a good chance of being achieved (as described below). Nonetheless, this pioneering approach can help to provide good outcomes for many patients.

Having recovered well, Lesley attended the 2014 London Marathon to cheer on her son-in-law, Adam, who was taking part. During the race, she noticed several of the runners wearing Ovacome T-shirts and decided to investigate. On doing so Lesley recognised the type of organisation that she could relate to and wanted to help. She became a member and, after attending the members' day meeting in May 2015, became a trustee of the charity the following year. Subsequently, Lesley has taken part in several of Ovacome' Survivors Teaching Students (STS) sessions (see chapter 6) as well as contributing her experience and wisdom in support of other cancer research organisations.

In the Desktop III trial, 407 patients with recurrent ovarian cancer were enrolled across the four-year period, 2010-2014 and randomly assigned to receive either chemotherapy alone (the standard treatment) or secondary surgery followed by chemotherapy. Each participant had to demonstrate specific medical factors and criteria to be enrolled in the trial, including: all first-occurrence cancer had been fully removed (complete resection) during original surgery; a period of at least six months post chemotherapy had passed prior to recurrence of the disease; less than 500ml of abdominal fluid (ascites) was evident at enrolment; the surgical team believed that all cancer could be removed during the secondary surgical procedure.

The full results of the trial were presented at an online medical conference of the American Society of Clinical Oncology, held May 29th-June 2nd 2020. They demonstrated a significant improvement in overall survival for those participants whose recurred cancer had been fully removed during secondary surgery. It seems likely that this approach will become the standard of care over time for patients who are fortunate enough to meet the success factors described.

Chapter 12

A Constant Presence

Throughout its 25-year history, Ovacome has seen many changes in just about every part of its operations. But there are two aspects of the charity that, whilst evolving and developing, have remained a constant presence throughout that period and form part of the bedrock of Ovacome: the medical advisory board (renamed the expert advisory panel in recent years) and the charity's patron, Jenny Agutter.

Ovacome received support from the medical profession from the very beginning. The late Professor Martin Gore and Professor Ian Jacobs attended the charity's launch event on September 15th 1996, gave informative speeches, and remained in touch thereafter providing expert advice as required. One year later, Ian Jacobs became a member of the committee of Ovacome and de facto medical advisor, writing articles for the newsletter. By 1998, a precursor to the full medical advisory board had been formed, consisting of both traditional and complementary healthcare professionals, to assist with the production of information provided by the charity to members and the wider community. And then, in 2000, the formal medical advisory board was established, consisting of 25 medical specialists, with Ian Jacobs appointed as its inaugural chairman. The role of the board was to advise the staff and trustees on all matters medical, including reviewing written factsheets and articles for the newsletter. Ian remained as chairman until 2003 when other work commitments resulted in him having to stand down.

One of Ian's colleagues on the founding board was Professor Sean Kehoe, who at that time was working at the John Radcliffe Hospital in Oxford, linked to the city's university. Through his work, Sean had met Louise Bayne, Ovacome chairperson and then CEO, as Louise often presented to, or attended meetings of, various ovarian cancer bodies. Eventually, Louise suggested to Sean that he become a trustee of the charity, an offer which he was happy to accept. He remains a trustee in early 2022.

Ovacome's heroines and heroes – Sean Kehoe's story

Sean was born in Dublin and attended Trinity College in the city where he studied medicine. On qualifying, he worked initially at the Baggot Street Hospital and then the Rotunda Hospital, both in Dublin, before moving to Galway in the west of Ireland where he obtained his Member of the Royal College of Gynaecologists qualification.

In 1990 he moved to the UK and took up the post of the Cancer Research Campaign (CRC) Gynaecological Cancer Research Fellowship at Birmingham University, completing his MD in ovarian cancer whilst there. Positions of lecturer, senior lecturer and, finally, honorary consultant, all at Birmingham University, followed. It was around this time that Sean first met Louise and became involved with Ovacome, joining the medical advisory board on its formation. In 2002, Sean moved from Birmingham University to take the foundation chair in gynaecological cancer at Oxford University where he developed the Oxford Gynaecological Cancer Centre. At the same time, he was appointed a fellow of St Peters College Oxford. As part of his research work, Sean launched the CHORUS trial (see chapter 4) that spanned a six-year period from 2004 to 2010 and involved multiple hospitals in the UK and New Zealand. It was to become a defining piece of work which, together with other studies, led to adjuvant chemotherapy becoming the commonest primary intervention for advanced ovarian cancer in the UK. In 2012 Sean was approached to rejoin Birmingham University in the prestigious role of Lawson-Tait (Dr Robert Lawson-Tait was a 19th century gynaecologist who pioneered pelvic and abdominal surgery and is often referred to, together with the American Dr James Marion Sims, as the father of gynaecology) chair of gynaecological cancer. His work there was selected as an impact case for a research excellence framework (REF) review of the university.

In April 2021 Sean was wooed back to Oxford as the professor of gynaecological cancer and lead for the Oxford gynaecological cancer service – he is adamant that this will be his last career move! His work has included: translational research, evidence-based medicine and clinical trials for gynaecological cancers, particularly ovarian cancer. He is a past president and current (2022) council member of the British Gynaecological Cancer Society.

On joining the medical advisory board, Sean worked behind the scenes, advising on articles and other documents of the charity for some years. And then, in December 2004, he hit the headlines with an article for Ovacome's newsletter that outlined the background, purpose and process of the CHORUS trial which had commenced earlier that year and for which he was the lead clinician. Sean became a regular presenter at members' day events, applying his Irish charm whilst covering a broad range of topics related to research and treatment of the disease. He also played a role in developing the UK consensus statement (see chapter 5), presenting at the conference that led to its publication in 2007.

By 2010, Sean had become the chairperson of a newly restructured medical advisory board consisting of 12 very senior oncologists and related health professionals. From that point on, Sean has been a regular face in the charity's newsletter/magazine providing important advice regarding the PETROC trial (see chapter 4A), the difficulties with screening for ovarian cancer and the feasibility of pregnancy following the disease, amongst other subjects. In 2014, a donation to Ovacome, from a patient of Sean's, provided funding for a research project that he leads, looking at how tumours change during the course of, and following treatment, with the goal of discovering improved further therapies.

Over the 11-year period since taking the chair, the board has continued to develop, grow and diversify under Sean's leadership and, in early 2022, consists of 23 healthcare professionals, specialising in oncology, nursing, physiotherapy, dietetics, general medicine, pathology, genetics, psychology and lifestyle medicine. Due to this impressive diversity of talent the board was renamed, the "expert advisory panel".

Over its 25-year existence, Ovacome has been able to obtain and rely on a wealth of specialist knowledge and experience from the members of its board/panel. In turn, this has played a major role in establishing Ovacome as a highly trusted and regarded charity throughout the UK and internationally. Current and past staff and trustees are immensely grateful for their diligence and hard work on the charity's behalf.

One spring day in 1996, a boy of five years old was attending his primary school like many thousands of others across the UK. During class, his teacher invited all the children to bring to school some photographs of their family to discuss. A few days later they did, and one young girl brought a picture of her mother, explaining to the class that about 18 months previously she had died of a disease called ovarian cancer. The young boy was sad and spoke to his mother about his school friend's loss. His mother reassured him as best she could that the girl, whilst very sad now, would get better over time.

The teacher involved was Alexandra Dargie (later to become the chairperson of Ovacome) and the mother of the young boy, Jenny Agutter.

Ovacome's heroines and heroes – Jenny Agutter's story

Jenny Agutter needs very little introduction, as her acting career is widely known internationally. Born in Taunton in 1952, her early childhood included spells in Germany,

Singapore and Cyprus as her father was an army officer. Back in the UK she attended ballet school and was chosen to dance in a Walt Disney production of the film Ballerina, *at the age of 11. In 1967 she played the role of Roberta (Bobbie) in the BBC's serialisation of* The Railway Children, *reprising the part three years later for a film version. The story, based on the book by Edith Nesbit, was a moving tale of a civil servant working in the Foreign Office (Bobbie's father) being wrongly convicted and imprisoned for spying, and Bobbie's role in helping to gain his freedom. Both serialisation and film helped to cement Jenny's growing reputation as an outstanding actor. Further roles followed, including the critically acclaimed film,* Walkabout, *and in 1971, her performance of Fritha in the BBC film* The Snow Goose *won her an Emmy award.*

At the age of 21, Jenny turned to theatre, joining the National Theatre for a season before moving to Hollywood, having been signed by MGM, to appear in the film Logan's Run. *Although based in Los Angeles, Jenny acted in both the USA and Europe, appearing in films including* The Eagle Has Landed, An American Werewolf in London *and* Equus, *for which she won a BAFTA. Jenny also continued her theatre career, becoming part of The Royal Shakespeare Company in the early 1980s. Having married Johan Tham and given birth to their son in 1990, Jenny moved back to the UK where she continued her acting career across many well-loved television, film and theatre productions, including playing the mother in a further adaptation of* The Railway Children, *for Carlton TV, in 2000.*

In January 2012 the first episode of a new series, titled Call the Midwife, *appeared on BBC One, with Jenny Agutter playing a lead role as Sister Julienne. It was an immediate success, scoring the highest ratings for a new BBC drama series in over a decade. Set in the East End of London in the 1950s and 60s, the programme was originally based on the memoirs of Jennifer Worth, a nurse who worked with an Anglican religious and nursing order at their convent in that part of the capital, although other historically based events have been included in the script. The series, each mostly of eight episodes, has run every year up to 2022 and is destined to continue beyond. It has won many accolades and awards since launch.*

Jenny's long acting career is well known and loved. Perhaps what is less well known is that Jenny is also a very strong supporter of several charities, including The Cystic Fibrosis Trust and Ovacome. In 2012 she was awarded an OBE for her services to charity.

Shortly after her pupils had brought in and talked about their family photographs, Alexandra Dargie read Sarah Dickinson's original article, published a month or two earlier in *Good Housekeeping* magazine and decided she would like to help (see chapter one). In doing so she contacted Jenny and asked her if she would be interested and prepared to offer support. Jenny agreed immediately as she believed strongly that more information and support was needed not just for those who contracted the disease but their families and friends. Jenny contacted Sarah and agreed to attend and speak at the launch event, becoming the charity's patron shortly thereafter. It was the start of a highly valuable and heart-warming relationship between Jenny and Ovacome that has remained steadfast over the entire history of the charity.

Jenny's work with Ovacome has touched on so many aspects of the charity's operations that it is difficult to overstate her contribution to the charity. She has attended several members' days, speaking at each, has appeared no fewer than 11 times on the front cover of Ovacome's newsletter/magazine, featuring many more times in the pages within. In 1997, Jenny opened the Ovacome-sponsored Ovarian Cancer Resource Centre at the Royal Marsden hospital in London and appeared in a video to boost knowledge of the disease that same year. A few years later she was photographed by Andy Scaysbrook as part of his first exhibition for Ovacome. Ten years later she was photographed again for his second exhibition, Holding on to Hope, attending the launch event. She played a prominent role in promoting Ovacome's BEAT campaign on the symptoms of ovarian cancer, speaking at the press conference that launched the programme and appearing on national TV to discuss the signs of the disease. She helped launch the charity's Survivors Teaching Students programme; has appeared and spoken at several Touch of Teal Tea with Ovacome events and played a lead role in promoting Ovacome's Teal Tips nail varnish campaign held during OCAM. Most recently, she has been a judge, together with her co-star from Call the Midwife, Stephen McGann, of Ovacome's highly successful short story writing competition. The list goes on.

Over a generation Jenny has supported Ovacome with enthusiasm, charm and grace. She is one of only two people to have been involved with the charity over its entire history, (the other being Sarah Dickinson's husband, Adrian) and Ovacome owes her an immense debt of gratitude for being such a star.

Chapter 13

DEALING WITH THE PANDEMIC

Nobody saw it coming of course. Why would they? All seemed very normal as people around the UK celebrated the arrival of 2020 in their time-honoured traditions. There had just been a general election and the big issue of the day was what would happen next with Brexit. Certainly, very few outside of the scientific community were thinking about the possibility of a global pandemic. Even when news of a new infection, called coronavirus, was first reported by the UK media in mid-January, apparently emanating from a fish market in a Chinese town that few people had heard of called Wuhan, there was little concern. The world had seen potentially very serious viruses before, dating back over decades, even centuries that had not been as bad as first feared. In the 2000s alone, the SARS virus, first seen in 2002, infected a little over 8,000 people, with 774 deaths. Toronto, Canada was particularly badly impacted. Later, in 2007/8 an avian flu outbreak, coded as H5N1, appeared to be very concerning and dominated headlines for a time, but ultimately claimed relatively few human lives. So far, so good.

But this was different, very different, as was about to become increasingly evident.

Ovacome's plans for the year were already well advanced in early January. Exciting initiatives for the newly opened Midlands office were in hand; models for the next Touch of Teal Tea had been confirmed and the event, the eleventh of its kind to be held, was set for September, as usual; OCAM (Ovarian Cancer Awareness Month) events for March were being slotted into members' diaries and there were high hopes of exceeding 2019's fund raising total. New initiatives targeted at minority groups and disadvantaged areas, where the latest consultation process had shown relatively poor outcomes for those developing ovarian cancer, were being identified and scheduled. The year was shaping up to be another of real progress for the charity.

As January progressed, news continued to be reported of increasing infection rates, and then deaths from coronavirus (SARS-CoV-2) in China. In late January the first case of coronavirus in the UK was reported, contracted by an individual who had returned recently from abroad. However, there had been no known transmission of the virus within the UK and it was hoped to keep it that way

As January moved to February it was full steam ahead for Ovacome's new Midlands hub. Laura Nott, the recently appointed hub coordinator, was busy meeting face to face with individuals affected by ovarian cancer, to understand their needs, and with local clinical nurse specialists to set up a local support group that would meet monthly. Supported by two local Ovacome ambassadors, Laura had arranged an inaugural TEAL walk to be held in Cannon Hill Park, Birmingham, on the 4th July. Ova to You meetings, and a health and wellbeing event were confirmed for later in the summer and autumn. A very exciting programme. She had even managed to arrange for Old Joe, the iconic bell tower at Birmingham University, to be lit up in the colour teal on March 2nd-4th as part of OCAM.

At the same time, Victoria, Ovacome's CEO, was getting very concerned at the daily news regarding coronavirus and began to think through worst case scenarios and how the charity would respond. Fortunately, Ovacome had already started the process of implementing additional remote access capabilities for members, based on the fact that significant numbers were unable to travel to physical events for one reason or another, not related to the pandemic.

Throughout February many more countries across the world began to report cases of coronavirus. In the UK small numbers of new infections were reported by the government and by the 27th of the month a total of 15 cases had been identified in England. All those infected had been abroad in recent days or weeks, including four who had been infected on a cruise ship in the Far East. And then, on February 28th, the first case believed to have been passed on within the UK, was reported by Chris Whitty (now Sir Chris Whitty), the chief medical officer of England. Whilst this was concerning, the rate of growth still appeared to be manageable as the UK government continued with the isolation of those confirmed to be infected, together with a "track and trace" approach to identify others who had been in contact with known cases.

At Ovacome, the first three weeks of March were a mixture of trying to maintain business as usual whilst urgently developing plans to continue to operate the charity in the face of what increasingly appeared to be a worldwide health crisis. OCAM events were launched at the beginning of the month, including the introduction of a new teal-coloured dress by Apricot, the fashion company working with Ovacome, plus a pendant necklace, both available in Apricot's stores and online. The virtual TEAL walk continued to gain momentum with another 50 brave souls signing up to add their sponsored footsteps to the overall target of walking the equivalent distance of the entire coastlines of the British Isles.

On March 1st the government announced 12 new cases of coronavirus, three times the highest daily total recorded to that point. Worryingly, at least one case could not be immediately traced to recent travel abroad or contact with another known case. It looked as if the genie was out of the bottle. Two days later the government's action plan for managing coronavirus was announced to the public. It set out a progressive four stage strategy to contain, delay, research and mitigate the virus with stage one being implemented immediately. By mid-March the UK had moved from the "contain" to the "delay" phase and many new initiatives to combat the spread of the virus had been announced, including most public venues being told to close. And then, on the evening of 23rd March, the prime minister took to the airwaves to announce to the public that "from this evening you must stay at home" in effect a full lockdown had been enacted of everything but essential services, shopping and minimal exercise.

It was at this point that Victoria's experiences of working under emergency conditions in Africa came to the fore. Immediately, telephone lines were switched to the staff team's homes and additional lines were added to cope with the anticipated increase in demand. Attention then focused on honing the plans that had already began to take shape in February and early March to move the entire operations of Ovacome online. Within seven days of lockdown the team had designed and begun delivering an alternative support programme, capable of caring for more people than ever before in the charity's history. That programme carried the apt title "Staying Connected". Staying Connected provided the platform for all of Ovacome's existing support groups to continue to meet online and for new groups to be added as needed. To help this effort, Ovacome teamed up with Ovarian Cancer Action (OCA), well known for their funding of research as well as awareness-raising, to run joint online workshops. It was the first time that two of the UK's major ovarian cancer charities had worked in such a partnership and heralded a more collaborative approach in the future, to the benefit of users of both organisations.

As 2020 progressed, Ovacome continued to refine some services and add new ones where required. The quarterly magazine moved a lot of its content to articles that helped readers deal with the many issues that they faced in a world where they could not meet with wider family or friends and, in many cases, were having to take measures to shield themselves from possible infection. Supportive topics included: taking positive steps to create safe places both physically and mentally; supporting the immune system when shopping was more difficult than normal and dealing with telephone or video based medical consultations. With gyms and swimming pools closed and daily walks restricted to one hour, Ovacome's online fitness classes became very popular. Never have tins of baked beans been put to such good use!

In the summer Ovacome launched its first ever short story writing competition. With significant prizes to be won the competition was open to all citizens of Great Britain, not just members of the charity. The theme for this first event was "Overcoming" which could be interpreted in any way by each writer. Each story could not exceed a maximum of 2000 words. A distinguished panel of three judges, from the world of authors and journalists, was appointed to judge a shortlist of three entries from over 100 received, reviewed and put forward by Ovacome staff and trustees. The ultimate winner, plus the two runners up, were announced in December to much fanfare. The competition had been a great success and was repeated the following year with the theme of "Connected". Nearly 200 entries were received and judged, this time by Ovacome's patron, Jenny Agutter and her fellow actor in *Call the Midwife*, Stephen McGann.

One year after opening, Ovacome's Midlands hub received a massive boost to its work as it received a grant of over £86,000 from the National Lottery Community Fund, specifically aimed at supporting local people during the coronavirus pandemic. The cash injection facilitated the recruitment of a further member of staff which, in turn, provided for the hub's team of two to target services at people based in Herefordshire, Shropshire, Staffordshire, Warwickshire and Worcestershire, in addition to the West Midlands. In a first for Ovacome, and with help from another, smaller but welcome cash grant from the Zurich Community Trust, handouts, posters, leaflets and a film all aimed at raising awareness of the disease, were distributed in Arabic, Bengali, Panjabi, Polish and Urdu as well as English. This important action was part of a commitment that Ovacome had made to increase its connection to minority groups and/or those living in deprived areas. Another initiative saw the Midlands hub join with several other support organisations including Sampad, a South Asian arts and heritage group, the European Welfare Association that supported Eastern Europeans, and an NHS trust that was looking at how black African and Caribbean people face barriers to accessing treatment and support. A very busy time for the Midlands based team.

As 2020 drew to a close, an arts and crafts group was added to the growing schedule of nationally available weekly online forums. Plus, a series of online clinical talks was scheduled with the first held in September, covering recent research into the disease. Future topics scheduled included a talk aimed at those with rarer forms of ovarian cancer, as well as sessions covering latest treatments and surgical techniques; all aimed at giving people the information they wanted and/or needed.

Setting up, expanding and running its own online support groups and forums, in a short time and under difficult circumstances, had been a triumph for the charity but Ovacome recognised also the importance of helping members establish their own local groups if they wished to. To help facilitate this, the staff team produced a 36-page support group booklet. Drawing on their own experience of moving all support services online in a short period of time, the booklet set out ideas and tips for setting up and running a successful group. The booklet and the ideas it contained were welcomed enthusiastically by many members, and new local groups began to pop up across the country.

If OCAM 2020 had been a challenge, the annual awareness and fundraising event was to be an even greater challenge in 2021 as many lockdown rules remained in place throughout the month. In recognition of this reality, Ovacome focused its efforts on virtual events and introduced the "41,000 acts for 41,000 people" campaign. The concept reflected the fact that, according to Cancer Research UK, some 41,000 women were living with ovarian cancer in the UK. The programme set a joint target of members and supporters carrying out 41,000 acts of awareness raising, whilst at the same time raising £41,000 for the charity, certainly ambitious in the circumstances.

Once again, people across the country responded magnificently with a plethora of events and activities taking place including: lighting public buildings in Derry, Northern Ireland in the colour teal; distribution of BEAT materials to family and friends; jewellery and other craft items being made and sold: members with birthdays in March asking for donations to be made to Ovacome in place of gifts; virtual raffles held, and many more. The virtual TEAL walk was a particular success throughout the month with people wearing their Ovacome T-shirts on their daily exercise walks. When the month was over, and the many, many donations totalled, an incredible £49,500, including over £15,000 from the virtual TEAL walk, had been raised, easily smashing the target set.

As spring turned to summer Ovacome launched one of its most important and thought-provoking information programmes to date. Titled "Give Her Time" it was a joint campaign between Ovacome, Ovarian Cancer Action and the pharmaceutical company GlaxoSmithKline. The campaign was developed following a survey among the ovarian cancer community, which sought to understand people's feelings about their future, and perspectives on the support received, following an ovarian cancer diagnosis. In a series of moving and candid videos, two Ovacome members, Samixa Shah and Kerry Burridge, shared what being given time by those around them had meant since their diagnosis. To support the campaign's messages, a document was put together, the Give Her Time Guide, containing some starting points for conversations between those diagnosed, loved ones, and healthcare professionals. The programme garnered significant interest and publicity with over 500 incidences of broadcast media and press coverage.

Towards the end of 2021 Ovacome introduced several new initiatives, including new specialist support groups; an enhanced programme of members reaching out to medical professionals that added to the enormous success of Survivors Teaching Students. Retitled "Patient Experience in Practice", the programme was online and able to reach a much wider audience of those wishing to understand the patient perspective first hand; new factsheets dealing with advanced ovarian cancer care; podcasts of members speaking openly about their experiences of the disease and hugely increased use of the main social media channels with almost daily Tweets, Instagram and Facebook postings. The year was ending on a high.

All this activity and transformation, in two years, from a blend of physical and online meetings and events to wholly virtual, home-based activity, was underpinned by two crucial factors. The first was the financial resilience of the charity that had been built up over the years and was able to withstand the inevitable reduction in funds received during the pandemic years. Second, the strength and cohesion of the staff team who demonstrated the most enormous commitment, ingenuity and stamina throughout.

Ovacome's heroines and heroes – the staff team who served for all or some of 2020/21

Alice, Anna, Eleanor, Elisa, Holly, Imogen, Kathy, Laura, Lee, Lois, Molly, Ruth, Victoria.

September 16th 2021. The day that Ovacome reached its first quarter of a century in existence as the first and foremost ovarian cancer support charity. To mark the occasion, Ovacome's autumn magazine carried several features dedicated to the historic date including an article by Adrian Dickinson, Sarah's husband and a current trustee of the charity. An iconic photograph of Sarah riding her bicycle at the start of the charity's launch day, 25 years previously, was reproduced proudly on the magazine's front cover.

Those 25 years had witnessed so many developments in just about every walk of life, from the beginnings of the internet to the smartphone, from posted mail to ubiquitous social media, through governments of different colours (including blended 2010-2015), from the petrol-driven Ford KA (chapter 1) to the electric vehicles of the 2020s, and so much more. Throughout all this change, Ovacome has learnt to adapt, to take advantage of the changes and developments for the benefit of its members and wider user base, and to grow and thrive. Never was this truer than during the awful years of global pandemic when so many felt vulnerable and isolated. But there is one element of the charity that has not changed; its dedication to the overriding vision of its founder and guiding spirit, Sarah Dickinson, to be the best possible support charity to all those impacted by Ovarian Cancer. That will never change.

Chapter 14

LOOKING TO THE FUTURE

What is the future of the diagnosis and treatment of ovarian cancer, and for the charities that, in one way or another, seek to offer hope and support?

Like many other causes, ovarian cancer has many charities dedicated to research, support or both. In the UK there are four larger charities and many smaller organisations, each carrying out valuable work in their own way. It is a valid question to ask, "Is this the best approach or would a smaller number of larger charities be an improvement?" This is a question that is asked of many areas in which charities play a role. For example, if you enter the question "are there too many cancer charities?" into an internet search engine you will find a wide range of opinion and comment.

The four larger charities focused on ovarian cancer (in fact, one of the four is focused on all five of the gynaecological cancers) each have somewhat different objectives; two largely focus on the funding of research into the disease, one (Ovacome) supports those with the disease, their families and friends, and one bridges both research and support. Additionally, there are other charities that focus on a wider range of cancers, including ovarian, for example, Cancer Research UK and Macmillan Cancer Support. Would it perhaps be better to consolidate the efforts of some of these charities into fewer, larger organisational structures? The answer is less clear than might be imagined. Merging organisations, whether companies or charities, presents many challenges: ensuring common motives of senior leaders new to each other, integrating different organisational cultures, combining the systems and processes of each. On the other hand, the benefits can be considerable, leading to improved cost structures, enlarged presence in the markets for both funding and talented staff, and reduced duplication of effort. In each case these potential risks and benefits must be weighed.

An alternative is for charities to partner in areas where there are common objectives and complementary skills, capabilities or experiences. There are many examples of ovarian cancer charities partnering with third parties and some of partnering together. A good example is the partnering of Ovacome and one of the other larger charities, Ovarian Cancer Action (largely focused on research) across several initiatives of each charity. Such cooperation can be expanded to the benefit of all.

As part of its oversight role, the Charity Commission seeks to ensure that there is not a proliferation of charities, all trying to serve the same purpose. Over the years, Ovacome has kept an open mind on these questions and to possible discussions with other charities. In doing so, the trustees have always kept paramount the overriding guiding principle of Sarah Dickinson's – that Ovacome should be a support charity to those who are impacted by this disease, either directly or indirectly. For 25 years Ovacome has been just that and, in early 2022, the existing trustees continue to uphold that simple goal.

It is not possible to predict the future – events over the past two years have certainly confirmed that truth. But for as long as ovarian cancer remains a disease that cannot be readily and consistently cured, and people affected by it need support, Ovacome will strive to help in every way it can; however long it takes.

And what of the disease? Are we closer to early detection and possible cure? The answers to these questions are more promising than at any time in the past.

As described in earlier chapters, the diagnosis of ovarian cancer has changed very little during the 25-year life of Ovacome. However, improved understanding of how ovarian cancer develops and research into new techniques for detecting the disease at an earlier stage (crucial to survival and cure) are leading to real hope of more timely detection.

Perhaps one of the most exciting areas of research into diagnostics in the early 2020s is work going on to identify changes to DNA that can be determined through a blood test. For example, work that has been going on for some years at Cambridge University (funded by Cancer Research UK), amongst others, has identified changes in a molecule found in DNA called p53 that may prove to be an early indicator of ovarian cancer (and others), particularly high-grade serous ovarian cancer (HGSOC). The research is ongoing.

On a larger scale, the NHS announced towards the end of 2020 that it intended to partner with Cancer Research UK and King's College London to launch the "Galleri" trial in England. This very exciting trial, a worldwide first, is based on a blood test developed by the Californian company, Grail, that has shown promising results in detecting many different types of cancer, including ovarian, at an early stage. It does this by looking for abnormal DNA from cancer cells circulating in the bloodstream. The trial, which aims to recruit around 150,000 participants in England, commenced in September 2021 and is ongoing. If successful it would be a major contributor to the goal of the NHS to identify three quarters of all cancers at an early stage when they are much more treatable.

Advances in understanding how ovarian cancer develops are also proving promising. As just one example, it is now widely acknowledged that most HGSOCs, which are the majority, develop first in the fallopian tubes, rather than the ovary itself. This knowledge can be helpful in guiding those with the BRCA mutation in considering whether to have their fallopian tubes and ovaries removed at the same time, triggering early menopause, or opt for fallopian tube surgery first (that does not result in early menopause), followed by ovary removal at a later date.

Recent work on drugs to treat ovarian cancer has, to a large extent, focused on the targeted treatments mentioned in chapter 11A. These drug therapies aim to inhibit a specific feature (or features) of the cancer cells' ability to divide and grow. Put simply, the development of tumour cells can take many different routes, or "pathways" which can now be identified by laboratory analysis. The targeted drugs act by disrupting, or inhibiting, the tumour cells pathway, hence halting, or at least slowing down, their progression.

PARP inhibitors were amongst the first of this class of drug and, whilst in common use today, continue to be researched and developed. Other types of inhibitors have also been discovered. For example, drugs known as ATR inhibitors have shown good results and are now being combined with PARP inhibitors to prolong survival further, particularly for those with HGSOC. For those with the much less common Low Grade Serous Ovarian Cancer (LGSOC), which represents around 5% of disease occurrence, a very recent trial of another type of drug, known as MEK inhibitors, have shown great promise. One such drug, named Trametinib, has been the subject of a recently completed, successful phase 2/3 trial, the results being published in *The Lancet* in February 2022. The evolution of inhibitor drugs is rapid and exciting, representing a major development in the medical response to ovarian, and other, cancers.

In addition to advanced drug therapies, surgical techniques continue to be developed. For example, the use of robotic surgery (laparoscopy) in the treatment of late stage ovarian cancer is being trialled at the Royal Surrey Hospital to determine if it is at least as effective as the traditional method (laparotomy) but with quicker recovery times.

All this work, plus much more, is improving, at an accelerating pace, the outlook for those unfortunate enough to contract the disease. Whilst we are not yet at the stage of being able to cure all, or most, ovarian cancers, we are, in the words of Professor Sean Kehoe, "Perhaps approaching the stage where the developments in therapies are so rapid that we may be able to facilitate a patient's long term survival with a high quality of life."

Let us hope that proves to be the case and that long term survival eventually equates to effective cure.

Acknowledgements

Few, if any, books are the work of just one person, and certainly this book was not; there are many people to thank for their help and support and I am pleased to acknowledge them here.

Throughout the project I was advised with great insight and wisdom by colleagues and friends who reviewed each chapter and gave me their candid comments, suggestions and ideas to improve the text. I offer heartfelt thanks to all of them. I am forever grateful to you.

In researching material for the book, I had the pleasure of interviewing (mostly over Zoom due to the pandemic of 2020/21) many inspiring people. Some are colleagues, others are eminent doctors and oncologists, still more are people who have contributed to Ovacome's work and achievements in one form or another over the years. Universally they gave their time, views, experiences and anecdotes freely and enthusiastically and I am indebted to each of them.

Finally, I want to thank my long suffering wife, the lovely Ann. Over an 18-month period she has put up with me locking myself away in my study for hours each week, never (well rarely!) complaining. Thanks, babe, I could not have done this without you.

Lightning Source UK Ltd.
Milton Keynes UK
UKHW010041291122
413021UK00013B/237/J